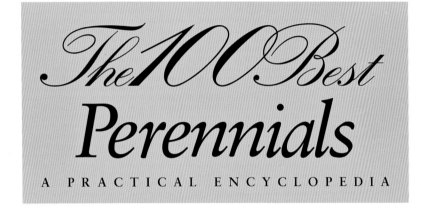

The 100 Best
Perennials

A PRACTICAL ENCYCLOPEDIA

Perennials

A PRACTICAL ENCYCLOPEDIA

PREVIOUSLY PUBLISHED AS PART OF *THE 400 BEST GARDEN PLANTS*

ELVIN MCDONALD

RANDOM HOUSE   NEW YORK

A Packaged Goods Incorporated Book

Published in the United States by
Random House, Inc.
201 E. 50th Street
New York, NY 10022

Conceived and produced by
Packaged Goods Incorporated
276 Fifth Avenue, New York, NY 10001
A Quarto Company

Text and photography by Elvin McDonald
Designed by Yasuo Kubota, Kubota & Bender

Library of Congress Cataloging-in-Publication Data
The 100 best perennials: a practical encyclopedia
Elvin McDonald.

p. cm.

Includes index.
ISBN 0-679-76028-8
1. Plants, Ornamental—Encyclopedias. 2. Plants,
Ornamental—Pictorial works. 3. Gardening—
Encyclopedias. 4. Gardening—Pictorial works.
I. Title. II. Title: The one hundred best perennials.
III. Title: A practical encyclopedia.

SB407.M26 1995
35.9— dc20 94-35385

Random House website address: http://www.randomhouse.com/
Color separations by Hong Kong Scanner Arts Int'l Ltd.
Printed and bound in Singapore by Khai Wah-Ferco Pte. Ltd.
98765432
First Edition

Acknowledgments

Dedicated to Marta Hallett

Thanks to the home team, pals, and friends, particularly:

Kristen Schilo, editor; Mary Forsell, copyeditor; Sarah Krall, assistant editor; Yasuo Kubota, designer; Tatiana Ginsberg, production manager; Amy Detjen, assistant production editor; Catherine San Filippo, proofreader; Lillien Waller, helping hand; Carla Glasser, agent; Douglas Askew, research; Tom Osborn, driver/gardener; Rosalind Creasy, focalizer; James R. Bailey, neighbor; Janis Blackschleger, telekineticist; Diane Ofner, gardening student; JoAnn Trial, scientist, and Don Trial, teacher; R. Michael Lee, architect; Charles Gulick, gardener; Michael Berryhill, poet; Linda Starr, head coach; Hila Paldi, body coach; Mark Inabnit, Publisher and Editor-in-Chief, *Houston Life*; David Walker, Editorial Director, *Houston Life*; Catherine Beason, angel unaware; Maria Moss, Executive Editor, *Houston Life*; David Warren, artist/gardenmaker; Audrey Scachnow, tweak expressionist; Christy Barthelme, envisionary; Tino and Richard, Stark Cleaning Services; Tony Williams, yard man; Dan Twyman, pruner; and Leslie Williams, cheering.

Elvin McDonald
Houston, Texas
January 1, 1997

Contents

Introduction

The one hundred plants that appear in these colorful pages represent my pick of the crop as a lifelong gardener and horticultural journalist. They are far from being the only "best" plants. Some vast families and categories certainly deserve more attention. Most assuredly, I am already growing the plants and assembling the photography for a sequel. One of the most wonderful aspects of gardening is that we can never know all of the plants. For this reason, dedicated gardeners will always experience the thrill of the hunt, the excitement upon discovering a flower or plant more beguiling than could have been imagined.

How to Read an Entry

Within this book, plants appear in alphabetical order by botanical genus name. If you know only the plant's common name, look for it in the Index. The botanical name and its suggested pronunciation are followed by the common name or names, many of which are interchangeable, and then by the plant's family name, appearing first in botanical Latin and finally in English. For example, plants of the genus *Digitalis* (botanical name) are commonly referred to as foxglove (common name). They are members of the Scrophulariaceae (botanical family name), or figwort family (common family name).

Within the entries, species names sometimes appear, where applicable. For instance, in the *Lychnis*, or campion, entry, the species names *L. coronaria* and *L. flos-jovis* appear. Both are broadly referred to as campion. Oftentimes, species do not have common names and, as a result, are known in the plant trade only by their botanical names.

In all, one hundred different plants are pictured in this volume, yet many more are actually named, a resource unto itself for tracking down worthwhile species and cultivars.

Within each entry, there is also a guide for cultivation:

Height/habit: Despite the inexactness of horticulture and botanical differences, I sum up here as much as can be said about a genus in as few words as possible.

Leaves: Many plants are appreciated for their foliage as much as—or even more so—than their flowers. Here I provide a succinct description of leaf shapes and characteristics.

Flowers: Dimensions, arrangement, and color and fragrance characteristics are noted.

Season: The plant's high season appears here.

When to plant: I have used the phrase "Set out transplants when available" for nearly all plants in the book. In other words, if a gardener shops regularly for plants, both through mail order and locally (at nurseries, garden centers, and plant auctions held by public gardens), they will be delivered or sold at approximately the correct planting time for that person's hardiness zone. Containerization, lightweight growing mediums, remarkably efficient distribution, and computerization have revolutionized the plant business. Yes, there are still plants shipped at the wrong time and local retailers who sell inappropriate choices, but on the whole, the system works.

I have also provided each plant's tolerance for cold and heat according to zone, as it appears on the United States Department of Agriculture's Plant Hardiness Zone Map (see page 112). (This information can also appear under "Season," if applicable.) However, please note that the U.S.D.A. map has traditionally been based on cold tolerance, not heat. Now the billion-dollar gardening industry is working to generate maps and zone awareness for heat as well as cold, also taking into account the relative dryness or wetness of a particular climate. To establish heat tolerance zones for this book, I have used a variety of references, including the catalogs of Louisiana Nursery, Wayside Gardens, and Yucca Do Nursery (see Resources). I have also consulted the books listed in the Bibliography, especially *A Garden Book for Houston* and *Hortica*. When in doubt, ask a neighbor who gardens for details about your hardiness zone. There are lots of variables and a host of gardeners who like nothing better than trying to succeed with a plant that is not rated for their zone.

Light: To prosper, most plants need strong light or some sun, in a site that affords air movement. Here, I provide specific light or shade requirements.

Soil: Most plants need well-drained soil that is kept evenly moist to on the dry side. There are rainy seasons when gardens are wet for long periods of time. If water stands for more than a few hours in your yard, this does not bode well for gardening—unless you are undertaking a water or bog garden. There are also dry seasons, and gardeners today generally subscribe to the concept of Xeriscaping: not to set in motion any garden that will require undue irrigation during normal times of drought.

Fertilizer: Generally speaking, 5-10-5 and 15-30-15 are good for flowering-fruiting plants. Timed-release 14-14-14 is an all-purpose, long-serving (up to a whole season from one application) fertilizer for a wide variety of plants. For acid-loving plants, choose 30-10-10 or chelated iron. Careful, consistent application of these or entirely organic fertilizers will result in vigorous growth.

Propagation: Lots of gardeners favor propagation over just about everything else done in the course of a gardening season. It is fun to see little seeds sprout and roots take hold from brown-looking cuttings. It is also practical if you have elaborate plantings in mind.

Uses: Under this heading, each plant's strong points are discussed, though you the gardener may find your own unique usages.

As much as I can provide detailed information about the art of gardening, you will be your own best teacher, a philosophy stated most eloquently in this old garden verse:

> *If you seek answers,*
> *leave your questions*
> *outside the garden gate.*

> *Elvin McDonald*
> *Houston, Texas   January 1, 1997*

Chapter One
The Perennial Garden

*M*any of the world's most breathtaking cultivated plants are classified as perennials, the mainstays of the garden. Technically speaking, a perennial is a plant that lives for more than two years; the term encompasses a great range of plants, including bulbs and trees. In this book, however, perennial flowers (often simply called perennials) and vines are the focus.

Locally adapted perennials and vines are all that you need to create an inviting outdoor "room." Vines can form the framework, covering fences and latticework (the "walls") as well as twining over arbors and pergolas (the "ceilings"). Perennials themselves are the "furnishings" and "accessories," perhaps intermingled with actual outdoor garden furniture.

The beauty of the perennial garden is that it lives on and on, returning every year without too much effort on the gardener's part. And there's always the ongoing quest for just the right perennial flowers and vines. Some gardeners like to grow only the newest introductions; others take pleasure in hunting down old garden flowers that are no longer common in commercial horticulture. Bringing a perennial garden to perfection can take years, but the pursuit is half the fun.

Planning and Designing the Perennial Garden

The most satisfactory perennial gardens are those planned according to the site and existing conditions. If the space is shaded, concentrate on perennials that do well in these conditions rather than languish. Daylilies, for example, will grow in shade but bloom little if at all. Primroses typically welcome lots of sun in cool spring weather, then prefer summer shade, making them ideal companions for deciduous trees and shrubs that do not leaf out until late in spring.

It helps to sketch ideas on graph paper, allowing each square to equal 1 foot (30 centimeters), or using any workable scale. Consider planting repetitive flower groupings, which lends a cohesive look to large spaces. A good gardener's rule of thumb is to set three plants or more together, in a triangle or a circle, so that an established clump can form as rapidly as possible.

No matter what the dimensions of your outdoor space, there is always a workable design scheme. A narrow border, say 3 feet (1 meter) wide by 40 feet (12 meters) long, might be organized around four 8-foot (2.4-meter) tepees, which both train vines and provide vertical accent. They can be placed equidistantly, beginning 5 feet (1.5 meters) in from each end, with about 7.5 feet (2.2 meters) between them. (Specific instructions on how to construct a tepee appear later in this chapter.) Growing in the border could be a diverse selection of perennials that bloom throughout the seasons.

Some gardeners design according to color scheme. They enjoy devising a different palette for every season or maintaining the same color of choice year-round. Once you've chosen a color, you needn't be bound to a particular hue.

For instance, a garden of blue flowers looks beautiful interplanted with perennials having silvery leaves. Other accents can come from flowers in any other color of the rainbow (complementary colors for blue include soft yellows or oranges as well as white), yet as long as blue and silver are used most abundantly, these serenely beautiful shades will dominate. Aside from color, there are many other design considerations in creating a perennial garden. Perennials and sociable vines are perfectly suited to mixing and matching with all other kinds of plants, from towering trees to alpine ground covers, and also respond well to being grown in containers. Here are some classic and contemporary design schemes:

Herbaceous Border

This style is associated with English gardens and involves planting densely. As one plant is fading, another is always just coming into bloom. Taller plants like peony, delphinium, and bleeding heart form the background, while medium-size plants like daylily, campion, and beardtongue bloom in the foreground. Planted so as to be clearly visible are the smaller perennials, such as lamb's ears and sedum.

Cottage Garden

Also associated with English gardens, the cottage style was originally a utilitarian garden of vegetables and herbs, with flowering and fragrant plants cultivated as well. Today, the cottage garden looks right at home in any geographical location. There are no rules for which types of plants look best, but classics include columbine, foxglove, lupine, primrose, evening primrose, and violet.

New American Garden

The idea for this style took root in a demonstration garden designed by Oehme van Sweden & Associates at the National Arboretum in Washington, D.C., under the directorship of Henry M. Cathey. By planting only locally adapted perennials, including ornamental grasses, they achieved a natural yet bold effect that highlights the seasonal glory of the garden. The key is to mass the plantings and not to use too many different species.

Xeriscape

This type of garden involves using only plants that will require very little irrigation during dry weather. Though pioneered by the Denver (Colorado) Water Department in the early 1980s, Xeriscaping is applicable everywhere, and plant selection varies to suit the particular locale.

Container Garden

For those whose gardening space is limited to a courtyard or deck, containers are the answer. They also appeal to gardeners who like to rearrange their plots frequently, adding pots here and there as they like—perhaps to punctuate the corners of an herbal knot garden or quickly brighten a corner of the yard where in-ground flowers have faded. Containers vary from clay and stone to wood, fiberglass, or even plastic (these retain moisture more efficiently than clay pots; if you want to hide the plastic, just slip them inside other, more attractive containers). Good perennial choices for containers are noted throughout Chapter

Two, but a quick list includes bleeding heart, monkshood, chrysanthemum, coralbells, bee balm, gayfeather, and coneflower.

Tepees

To train vines and discipline unwieldy perennials, tepees are useful and decorative. Insert three or four bamboo stakes 6 to 8 feet (1.8 to 2.4 meters) long about 6 inches (15 centimeters) deep in the ground, 1.5 feet (45 centimeters) apart. Tie the tops together. The result will be a tripod or quadripod. Smaller or larger tepees are also possible. Sometimes it helps to fill the bottom interior of the structure with pea-vine brush, which allows tendril-climbing or twining vines to take hold.

Soil Preparation

Some perennials thrive in boggy conditions—perhaps by a body of water or along the banks of a stream—and they are noted throughout Chapter Two. Most, however, require soil that is well drained and that contains sufficient humus to give roots air and a reserve of moisture. If the endemic soil has a high clay or sand content, add 5 to 6 inches (12.5 to 15 centimeters) of well-rotted compost and mix thoroughly into the top 5 to 6 inches (12.5 to 15 centimeters) of soil.

If drainage is poor or your region experiences seasons of high heat and high humidity, such as along the Gulf Coast of the United States, raised planting beds are essential. These can be built of wood, landscape timbers, railroad ties, concrete blocks, or whatever material seems appropriate. The beds should be at least 6 to 8 inches (15 to 20 centimeters) deep and can then be filled with a mixture of endemic soil, well-rotted compost, and possibly sphagnum peat moss or leaf mold. Adding sand to the soil also helps drainage.

Theoretically, a perennial garden bed that is once or twice annually top-dressed with well-rotted compost will not need any additional fertilizer. However, in practice, gardeners often like to side-dress with 5-10-5 granules in the spring and again at midsummer. It is also common practice to mix in 14-14-14 or similar timed-release pellets at planting time.

Buying and Planting Perennials

Gardeners have several options in purchasing perennials. They can choose from container-grown perennials at their local nursery—a very convenient method, as it allows for planting whenever you wish, from spring through fall in the North and year-round in zones 8 through 9. It is also a great help to purchase plants in bloom, so you'll know exactly what you're getting.

To plant a potted perennial, first water the ground thoroughly. Dig a hole a bit larger than the pot. Add compost to the hole to spur new plant growth. Turn over the pot and tap it lightly. The rootball should give easily, but if it does not, loosen the edges with a knife. Set the whole rootball in the hole with its top just beneath the surface of the soil. Water again, and add a little fertilizer if you wish.

The second option is to order special varieties and cultivars from growers. They will ship at the proper time in spring for planting, usually sending the semidormant roots of herbaceous perennials. Plant these according to the enclosed directions. For a list of such growers, refer to the Resources section of this book.

Another possibility is to plant from seeds, which can be obtained both at the nursery and through the mail-order catalogs. You can also collect seeds from your own garden (though many perennials do not grow "true" from seed, and the plant you grow might not resemble the parent). Seeds from catalogs are usually planted in spring; seeds from your own plants go into the ground toward the end of summer, when they would naturally plant themselves. Some gardeners opt for raising perennial seeds in a cold frame, to protect them from the elements; after they are well developed (after several months), they transplant them to a garden bed.

Caring for Perennials Throughout the Seasons

Catalog writers and garden book publishers may refer to them as "carefree," but in fact hardly any living plant is truly carefree. Throughout their long growing season, perennials should be given a bit of care nearly every day. Besides general training, tidying, and deadheading, there is also watering in time of drought, especially early in the season when roots are getting established; fertilizing if the soil is impoverished; and occasionally taking action against invasive weeds or insects. Except for the longest-lived perennials, such as herbaceous peony and baptisia, most perennials benefit from being dug and divided at least once every four or five years. Otherwise they are inclined to crowd themselves out in the centers.

You'll know it's time when you see new, stronger roots wrapping around the crown of the plant. Division rejuvenates the plant and is done before or after flowering. Most gardeners divide spring or summer bloomers in late summer to early fall and late bloomers the following spring. To divide, push two spading forks into the plant's crown and then pull the handles away from each other to detach the roots. Then pull the clump apart and replant young rootstocks.

Stems of tip cuttings are an expedient means of propagating perennials in spring and summer. A new plant grown this way will be exactly like the one from which it came. Use healthy, vital growth, usually at some medium age between the newest (at the tips) and the oldest (toward the base of the plant), and take cuttings 4 to 5 inches (10 to 12.5 centimeters) long.

Remove at least one or two sets of leaves from the base; roots develop at the nodes where leaves grew before. If leaves remaining at the top of the cutting are large and inclined to floppiness or wilting, cut them back by one-half to two-thirds. This reduces stress on the cutting and helps it concentrate energy on developing new roots. Set each cutting 1 to 2 inches (2.5 to 5 centimeters) deep in moist rooting medium. Bright light, moderate temperatures (55 to 75°F [13 to 24°C]), even moisture, and good circulation of moist air help cuttings take hold.

Perennials having fleshy roots often can be propagated by setting lengths 2 to 4 inches (5 to 10 centimeters) long in prepared soil in fall or early spring, about 1 inch (2.5 centimeters) deep. Perennials that can be propagated from root cuttings include anemone, Oriental poppy, trollius, phlox, echinops, and verbascum.

Essential Tools

Aside from the usual trowel, Cape Cod weeder, and three-pronged cultivator, the perennial gardener seldom has a better friend than the border spade or woman's perennial spade. This works perfectly for digging holes to accommodate plants from gallon-size plastic pots, as well as for quick division and transplanting chores. For staking and tying, it also helps to have twigs and brush cut from the property, bamboo canes, and various means of tying, such as raffia, jute, and plastic-and-wire twist-ties.

Year-round Gardening Calendar

Here is a calendar of seasonal reminders:

SPRING:

Cut back and clean up dead growth as the weather warms and there is little danger of further killing frost.

Set brush stakes ("pea-vine sticks") over and around clumps of perennials that grow tall later—peonies, summer phlox, heliopsis.

Side-dress with 5-10-5 fertilizer.

Till and prepare soil in garden beds and top-dress with fertilizer.

Sow seeds of perennials or transplant seedlings after danger of frost has passed.

Bring transplants to the garden.

Mulch with organic matter.

Divide late-flowering perennials.

Start a garden watering schedule, watering soil thoroughly yet infrequently as a conservation measure. To check if soil needs to be watered, see if it feels dry 3 to 4 inches (7.5 to 10 centimeters) down.

Bring spring perennial bouquets indoors.

Deadhead spent blooms.

SUMMER:

Continue weeding and deadheading.

Water deeply in times of drought or, alternatively, rely on locally adapted perennials and mulching to conserve resources.

Plant seeds of perennials collected from your own garden.

Bring summer perennial bouquets indoors.

FALL:

Continue watering, weeding, and deadheading.

In late fall, side-dress with several inches of well-rotted compost or rotted manure. Left to cure over winter, this treatment enhances microlife in the soil and results in perennial plantings that are stronger and inherently more resistant to predatory insects and diseases.

Divide spring-flowering plants about a month before ground freezes.

Do not cut perennial stems and grasses to the ground—throughout the winter, they will provide cover for animals and add interest to the landscape.

Bring late summer/early fall perennial bouquets indoors.

WINTER:

Begin designing your perennial garden on paper.

Order everything you'll need: tools, seeds, flats, starting mixes.

Start perennial seeds indoors.

In the North, press back into the earth any crowns of perennials that may have been heaved up by alternate freezing and thawing.

ACHILLEA
(ack-il-LEE-ah)

Yarrow

COMPOSITAE; daisy family

Height/habit: Lacy, often finely cut leaves in a basal rosette from which the flowering stems arise, 1–4 ft. (30–122 cm.) high/wide.

Leaves: Pinnately dissected, each 2–10 in. (5–25 cm.) long by one-third as wide, growing alternately or in a basal rosette, green to gray-green.

Flowers: Corymb-forming, 1–6 in. (2 .5–15 cm.) across, 1–4 ft. (30–122 cm.) high, rising above the foliage; white, yellow, red, orange, or pink. Hybrids of *A. millefolium* and *A. taygetea* have expanded the color range for this type into pastels. Prompt deadheading encourages a second blooming.

Season: Summer.

When to plant: Start seeds indoors 8–12 weeks ahead of planting-out weather for blooms in the same season; set transplants when available. If yarrow grows wild on your property, transplant some of the choicest clumps to your cultivated garden. If watered and shaded at first they can be transplanted while in bloom. Cold-hardy zones 2–3, heat-tolerant through zones 9–10.

Light: Sunny to half-sunny. Plants in light soil receiving full sun will grow barely one-third the size of those in rich soil receiving a half day of sun.

Soil: Well drained, moist to slightly on the dry side.

Fertilizer: 5-10-5.

Propagation: Sow seeds or divide plants having several crowns in spring or fall. Achilleas are at their best in the second and third seasons; rejuvenate by digging, dividing, and replanting only the strongest of the newer growths every 2–3 years.

Uses: Beds, borders, pots, cutting fresh or dried.

ACONITUM
(ack-oh-NEYE-tum)

Monkshood; Aconite

RANUNCULACEAE; buttercup family

Height/habit: Leafy shoots from the ground become flowering plants 3–6 ft. (1–1.8 m.) high/wide that often benefit from staking. Caution: Members of the Aconitum genus are poisonous.
Leaves: Finely cut, basal, similar to those of delphinium; 6–8 in. (15–20 cm.) across.
Flowers: Tubular to hood-shaped, 1–2 in. (2 .5–5 cm.) long/wide, growing in spikes showing well above the leaves; white through all shades of blue to purple; *A. anthora* is yellow and blooms before the blue types; *A. compactum* is pale pink.

Season: Midsummer through fall. Cold-hardy to zones 4–5 but diminished by heat zones 8–9 and warmer.
When to plant: Set transplants when available and do not disturb unless divisions are wanted.
Light: Sunny to half-sunny.
Soil: Humusy, well drained, moist to wet. Monkshood often colonizes moist banks.
Fertilizer: 5-10-5.
Propagation: Sow seeds outdoors in the fall for germination the following spring; seedlings bloom the third season. Established clumps can be divided when the soil is workable in spring.
Uses: Beds, borders, pots, cut flowers.

AJUGA
(ah-JEW-gah)

Bugleweed; Carpet Bugle

LABIATAE; mint family

Height/habit: Ground-hugging plants that form a dense mat, spreading via runners.
Leaves: Spatula-shaped, 1–4 in. (2.5–10 cm.) long by one-third as wide, mostly in basal rosettes; depending on the cultivar they may be green, burgundy, or silver.
Flowers: Compact spikes rising above the leaves, 3–6 in. (7.5-15 cm.) long; blue or white.
Season: Flowers in spring; foliage attractive most of the year. Cold–hardy zone 3; heat-tolerant through zone 9.

When to plant: Set transplants when available.
Light: Full sun (in cooler climates) to nearly full shade.
Soil: Humusy, well drained, moist.
Fertilizer: 5-10-5.
Propagation: Divide in spring or early fall or remove runners that have started to root.
Uses: Border edging, ground cover, outdoor pots.

ALCHEMILLA
(al-kem-MILL-ah)

Lady's Mantle

ROSACEAE; rose family

Height/habit: Low-mounding or carpeting herbs rarely exceeding 1 ft. (30 cm.) even in bloom, spreading 2–3 ft. (61–90 cm.) wide.

Leaves: Velvety, rounded, lobed, cut at the edges, 1–5 in. (2.5–12.5 cm.) wide; dewlike droplets from normal guttation (exudation of water from leaves) appear mornings on these beautiful leaves.

Flowers: Loose, feathery panicles 15 in. (38 cm.) high; yellow-green.

Season: Leaves from spring until fall frost; flowers midsummer. Cold-hardy zone 3, sometimes heat-tolerant through zone 8.

When to plant: Set transplants when available.

Light: Sun (cooler climates) to part shade.

Soil: Humusy, well drained, moist.

Fertilizer: 5-10-5.

Propagation: Sow seeds or divide in spring.

Uses: Edging, ground cover, outdoor pots.

ANEMONE
(ah-NEM-oh-nee)
Windflower; European Pasqueflower; Japanese Anemone

RANUNCULACEAE; buttercup family

Height/habit: Bushy, upright, 1–4 ft. (30–122 cm.) high/wide.

Leaves: Deeply cut, mostly from the base, plain green except notably silver-haired in European pasqueflower (*A. pulsatilla*), 1–2 ft. (30–61 cm.) high/wide.

Flowers: Single to double, often with showy stamens, 1–3 in. (2.5–7.5 cm.) across, on slender, graceful stems, 1–4 ft. (30–122 cm.) high; white, pink, mauve, blue, purple, or rosy carmine.

Season: Spring for the wind-flower (*A. canadensis* and *A. pulsatilla*); late summer through fall for the Japanese anemone (*A. hupehensis japonica*). Cold-hardy zones 3 (with protection) through 6, heat tolerance questionable zones 8 and warmer.

When to plant: Set transplants when available, ideally spring for those that bloom in the fall and fall for those that bloom in the spring.

Light: Full sun to part shade.

Soil: Humusy, well drained, moist.

Fertilizer: 5-10-5.

Propagation: Sow seeds or divide in spring or fall.

Uses: Beds, borders, outdoor pots, cut flowers.

AQUILEGIA
(ack-kwill-EE-jee-ah)

Columbine

RANUNCULACEAE; buttercup
family

Height/habit: Tidy clumps of
graceful, fernlike, blue-green
leaves, 1–2 ft. (30-61 cm.)
high/wide, surmounted by
elegant, wiry stems that bear
the showy flowers.
Leaves: Cut, mostly growing
from the base of the plant,
6–18 in. (15–45 cm.) long/wide,
from pale, bright green to quite
a glaucous blue-green. Leaf
miners often disfigure the leaves
but this seldom hurts the plants.
Flowers: Often have noticeable
spurs that give them a light,
airborne quality, 2–4 in.
(5–10 cm.) across; most colors,
typically bicolored.

Season: Spring. Cold-hardy
through zone 5; 'Hinckley's
Yellow' is the most reliable
columbine for humid, hot
gardens zone 8 and warmer.
When to plant: Set transplants
when available, ideally in early
spring or fall.
Light: Sun to half shade.
Soil: Humusy, well drained,
moist.
Fertilizer: 5-10-5.
Propagation: Sow seeds in
spring or fall, or transplant self-
sown seedlings (note: named
hybrid cultivars do not grow
true from seeds).
Uses: Beds, borders, rock gardens, pots, cut flowers. Also for
wild gardens and naturalizing:
A natural stand of blue-and-
white *A. caerulea* is particularly
memorable. Another favorite
for naturalizing is the delicate
red-and-yellow Canadian
columbine (*A. canadensis*).

ARABIS
(AIR-abb-iss)

Rock Cress

CRUCIFERAE; mustard family

Height/habit: Mounding
or mat-forming, 6–12 in.
(15–30 cm.) high by several
times as wide.
Leaves: Small, gray-green,
mostly toward the base; 2–3 in.
(5–7.5 cm.) long.
Flowers: 4-petaled (occasionally doubled in choice cultivars),
each to .5 in. (1.25 cm.) across,
but appearing in such profusion that the foliage is nearly
obscured; white, pink, or rose.

Season: Early spring flowers.
When to plant: Set transplants
when available, best in early
spring or early fall. Cold-hardy
through zones 5–6 but intolerant of hot/humid summer conditions zones 8 and warmer.
Light: Full sun half day or
more.
Soil: Well drained, moist in
spring; keep on the dry side in
summer.
Fertilizer: 5-10-5.
Propagation: Sow seed, divide,
or take stem tip cuttings in
spring or fall.
Uses: Edging, spilling from a
rock wall, borders, outdoor
pots with bulbs in spring.

ARTEMISIA
(art-eh-MEE-zee-ah)

Wormwood; Silver-king; Tarragon

COMPOSITAE; daisy family

Height/habit: Clump-forming to colonizing, mostly upright, gray-leaved plants, 1–4 ft. (30–122 cm.) high/wide.

Leaves: Finely cut in many species, including wormwood (*A. absinthium*), entire in *A. albula* (silver-king) and *A. dracunculus* (tarragon). The leaves typically have a pungent odor when brushed against; those of 'Powis Castle' smell particularly sweet.

Flowers: Inconspicuous and tiny if present at all.

Season: Foliage color from spring until frost and even beyond.

When to plant: Set transplants when available, ideally in spring. Generally cold-hardy through zone 4. Silver-king and 'Powis Castle' adapt to humid, hot weather through zone 9.

Light: Sun half day or more.

Soil: Well drained, moist to on the dry side.

Propagation: Divide in spring or take stem tip cuttings.

Uses: Beds, borders, pots, cutting fresh or dried. These sturdy plants are chosen mostly for their silvery effect that, when repeated throughout a garden, helps pull together many different flower colors and forms.

ARUNCUS
(ah-RUNK-us)
Goat's Beard
ROSACEAE; rose family

Height/habit: Large clumps of compound leaves crowned by tiny flowers in spikes, 5–6 ft. (1.5–1.8 m.) high/wide.

Leaves: Compound, graceful, even feathery, 12–15 in. (30–38 cm.) long/wide, medium to dark green.

Flowers: Spikes 1–1.5 ft. (30–45 cm.) long rising above the foliage; flowers tiny but abundant; creamy white.

Season: Flowers early to mid-summer.

When to plant: Set transplants when available, ideally fall or early spring. Cold-hardy through zone 5; sometimes grows in hot, humid conditions in zone 9 and warmer.

Light: Half-sunny to half-shady.

Soil: Humusy, well drained, moist.

Fertilizer: 5-10-5.

Propagation: Divide in spring or transplant self-sown seedlings.

Uses: Borders, accents, large outdoor pots, streamside.

ASARUM
(ah-SAY-rum)

Wild Ginger

ARISTOLOCHIACEAE; birthwort
family

Height/habit: Low, ground-
covering, 6–10 in. (15–25 cm.)
high/wide.
Leaves: Heart-shaped, shiny,
dark green, to 5 in. (12.5 cm.)
across.
Flowers: Inconspicuous, purplish brown, borne under the
leaves.
Season: *A. canadense* is deciduous; the other species cultivated
are evergreen.

When to plant: Set transplants
when available. *A. canadense* is
cold-hardy through zone 3, the
evergreen species variously
zones 4–6. Questionably heat-
tolerant zone 8 and warmer.
Light: Half to full shade.
Soil: Humusy, well drained,
moist.
Fertilizer: 5-10-5.
Propagation: Divide roots in
spring or summer.
Uses: Edging or ground cover
in wild, woodland, or rock
gardens.

ASCLEPIAS
(az-KLEEP-ee-az)

Milkweed; Butterfly Weed; Bloodflower

ASCLEPIADACEAE; milkweed family

Height/habit: Upright, bushy, 2–5 ft. (61–150 cm.) high/wide.

Leaves: Narrow, 2–6 in. (5–15 cm.) long.

Flowers: Umbels 2–3 in. (5–7.5 cm.) across at the stem tips above the leaves; yellow, orange, red, pink, white, often bicolored.

Season: Summer.

When to plant: Set transplants when available; take care planting so as to disturb the roots as little as possible. Butterfly weed (*A. tuberosa*) cold-hardy through zone 3, also heat-tolerant through zone 10. Bloodflower (*A. curassavica*) tropical: Grow in ground zones 9–10, elsewhere in pots that can winter indoors in a warm place.

Light: Sun half day or more.

Soil: Well drained, moist. *A. tuberosa* often grows wild in sandy soil.

Fertilizer: 5-10-5.

Propagation: Sow seeds or take root cuttings in spring.

Uses: Beds, borders, outdoor pots, butterfly gardens.

ASTER
(AST-er)

Michaelmas Daisy; New England and New York Asters

COMPOSITAE; daisy family

Height/habit: Bushy mounds 1–6 ft. (30–180 cm.) high/wide.
Leaves: Simple, alternate, narrow, 2–6 in. (5–15 cm.) long, dark green.
Flowers: Daisylike, each from .25–4 in. (.63–10 cm.) across, in loose heads, often hiding the leaves; red, rose, pink, white, blue, purple, or mauve.
Season: Summer for *A.* x *frikartii*; late summer until fall frost for most cultivars of New England aster (*A. novae-angliae*) and New York aster (*A. novi-belgii*).

When to plant: Set transplants when available, ideally in spring as soon as the soil can be worked. Cold-hardy through zones 5–6 and surprisingly tolerant of hot, humid summers through zones 8–9.
Light: Full sun to light shade.
Soil: Humusy, well drained, moist.
Fertilizer: 5-10-5.
Propagation: Divide or take cuttings in spring or early summer. Divide and replant every third or fourth year to keep the plants vigorous. Seeds planted in spring bloom first the following year but produce unpredictable sizes and colors.
Uses: Beds, borders, outdoor pots, cut flowers.

ASTILBE
(az-TILL-be)

False Goat's Beard

SAXIFRAGACEAE; saxifrage family

Height/habit: Tidy clumps 18–40 in. (45–100 cm.) high/wide.

Leaves: Compound and divided, 6–12 in. (15–30 cm.) long/wide; some deeply cut and feathery, bronzy to dark green.

Flowers: Showy panicles 2–4 in. (5–10 cm.) long or more consisting of tiny flowers rising above the leaves; white, pink, rose, red, lavender, or purple.

Season: Flowers about 4–6 weeks at the beginning of summer; foliage attractive spring through fall.

When to plant: Set transplants when available, ideally in spring or early fall. Cold-hardy through zone 5 but intolerant of hot, humid summers zone 9 and warmer.

Light: Half sun to half shade.

Soil: Humusy, well drained, moist.

Fertilizer: 5-10-5. Yellowish leaves with green veins could indicate a need for lower pH; treat by fertilizing with 30-10-10 or applying chelated iron according to product label instructions.

Propagation: Divide in spring.

Uses: Beds, borders, outdoor pots, cut flowers.

AURINIA
(aw-RINN-ee-ah)

Basket-of-gold Alyssum

CRUCIFERAE; mustard family

Height/habit: Sprawling, trailing, or cascading, 6–12 in. (15–30 cm.) high and several times as wide.

Leaves: Narrow, spatula-shaped, to 5 in. (12.5 cm.) long, gray-green.

Flowers: About .25 in. (.63 cm.) across in heads that completely cover the plants; pale to vivid yellow.

Season: Early to midspring. Cut or shear off the flower heads after bloom.

When to plant: Set transplants when available. Cold-hardy through zone 4, heat-tolerant through zone 8.

Light: Sun half day or more.

Soil: Well drained, moist to on the dry side.

Fertilizer: 5-10-5.

Propagation: Take stem cuttings in spring or summer or sow seeds in spring.

Uses: Edging at front of border, spilling over or from a rock wall, outdoor pots.

BAPTISIA
(bap-TIZ-ee-ah)

False Indigo

LEGUMINOSAE; pea family

Height/habit: Upright, shrub-like, to 3 ft. (90 cm.) high x 2 ft. (61 cm.) wide.

Leaves: Compound leaflets arranged in groups of 3; blue-green.

Flowers: Lupinelike in sprays at the top of the plant; dark blue in *B. australis*, yellow in *B. tinctoria* (both known as false indigo).

Season: Late spring through early summer for *B. australis*, all summer for *B. tinctoria*.

When to plant: Set transplants when available, ideally spring or fall. Cold-hardy zone 4, heat-tolerant zone 9.

Light: Sun half day or more.

Soil: Humusy, well drained, moist; tolerates drought but not alkaline pH.

Fertilizer: 5-10-5.

Propagation: Sow seeds in fall or divide in spring. Established plants can be left undisturbed indefinitely.

Uses: Beds, borders, wild gardens, dried seedpods for winter arrangements.

BERGENIA
(ber-JEE-nee-ah)

Megasea

SAXIFRAGACEAE; saxifrage family

Height/habit: Low clumps of bold foliage 1–1.5 ft. (30–45 cm.) high/wide.

Leaves: Evergreen, rounded, wavy at the edges, to 10 in. (25 cm.) long/wide; bright green to glowing burgundy, depending on the variety and the time of year.

Flowers: Loose panicles, 1–1.5 ft. (30–45 cm.) high, standing above the leaves; purplish red, bright pink, or white.

Season: Flowers early to mid-spring, leaves attractive at most times.

When to plant: Set transplants when available. Cold-hardy zones 2–3, heat-tolerant zone 9 (*B. crassifolia*, favored in California, is rated zones 3–10).

Light: More sun in cooler climates, more shade in hot places.

Soil: Sandy, well drained, moist.

Fertilizer: 5-10-5.

Propagation: Divide or sow seeds in spring.

Uses: Beds, borders, rock gardens, ground cover, pathway edging, leaves for flower arrangements.

BOUGAINVILLEA
(boog-in-VILL-ee-ah)

Paper Flower

NYCTAGINACEAE; four-o'clock
family

Height/habit: Potentially large
(to 60 ft. [18 m.] in some areas)
evergreen woody vines with
sharp spines along the stems.
Leaves: Smooth, alternate,
tapering at the base, to 4 in.
(10 cm.) long.
Flowers: Very small 5-lobed
trumpets, each barely .25 in.
(.63 cm.) wide; pale yellow to
white, several arising from the
center of each showy, papery,
long-lasting bract that can be
greenish white, yellow, orange,
peach, or brilliant magenta,
often profuse.
Season: Virtually everblooming
zone 10 and warmer; zone 9
and colder blooms appear
throughout most of summer
or, conversely, may soak up
energy outdoors all through
warm weather, then give it back
in the form of winter flowers
in a sunny garden room.

When to plant: Set transplants
when available, outdoors when
temperatures are above 50°F
(10°C). Take care not to over-
water in cool temperatures or
when the roots have been disturbed. Reliably winter-hardy
outdoors zone 10; elsewhere
move to a frost-free location as
necessary, with plenty of sun
and air circulation.
Light: Sun half day or more.
Soil: Well drained, moist to
quite dry.
Fertilizer: Potassium- (potash-)
rich blend, such as 12-12-17.
Propagation: Take stem
cuttings in spring. Training
and pruning techniques are
similar to those of wisteria:
First establish the permanent
framework, then cut back to
spurlike growths in the fall or
after a heavy flowering.
Uses: Zone 10 and warmer, use
as a screen or fence and arbor
cover; zone 9 and colder, keep
pots outdoors in frost-free
weather.

CAMPANULA
(kam-PAN-yew-lah)

Bellflower

CAMPANULACEAE; bellflower family

Height/habit: Variously upright or trailing, 1–4 ft. (30–122 cm.) high/wide.

Leaves: Often clustered in a basal rosette, oblong to lanceolate, to 8 in. (20 cm.) long.

Flowers: Bell-shaped, in racemes, also solitary or in heads, spikes, or panicles, 1–3 in. (2.5–7.5 cm.) across; blue, white, and occasionally pink or rose. Garden favorites include Carpathian bellflower (*C. carpatica*), Adriatic bellflower (*C. elatines*, an outstanding rock and wall plant), clustered bellflower (*C. glomerata*), peach-leaf bellflower (*C. persicifolia*), chimney bellflower (*C. pyramidalis*), and bluebells-of-Scotland (*C. rotundifolia*). Deadheading encourages a second blooming.

Season: Summer.

When to plant: Start seeds indoors 8–12 weeks ahead of planting-out weather for blooms in the second season; set transplants when available. Cold-hardy zone 3, heat-tolerant through zones 7–8.

Light: Sunny to half-sunny.

Soil: Well drained, evenly moist.

Fertilizer: 5-10-5.

Propagation: Sow seeds in spring or summer or divide plants having several crowns in spring or fall. Campanulas are at their best in the second and third seasons; rejuvenate by digging, dividing, and replanting only the strongest of the newer growths every 3–4 years.

Uses: Beds, borders, rock gardens, outdoor pots, cut flowers.

CAREX
(KAIR-ex)

Sedge

CYPERACEAE; sedge family

Height/habit: Upright to cascading grassy clumps, to 1 ft. (30 cm.) high/wide.

Leaves: Grasslike, to 1 ft. (30 cm.) long; extremely narrow in some varieties; green, gold, white, brown, buff to apricot.

Flowers: Brownish spikelets at the tips of leaflike stems. Grown mostly for foliage color and texture.

Season: Cultivated sorts are attractive for foliage effect from spring through fall, occasionally all winter.

When to plant: Set transplants when available. Cold-hardiness varies, zones 5–7; heat-tolerance for most through zone 9.

Light: Sunny to half-sunny.

Soil: Moist to boggy.

Fertilizer: 5-10-5.

Propagation: Divide established clumps in spring.

Uses: Beds, borders, pots. Ideal for pond banks and stream edges.

CENTRANTHUS
(sen-TRANTH-us)
Valerian; Jupiter's Beard
VALERIANACEAE; valerian family

Height/habit: Bushy, upright, 2–3 ft. (61–90 cm.) high/wide.
Leaves: Gray-green, 3–4 in. (7.5–10 cm.) long, mostly toward the lower half of the plant.
Flowers: Dense clusters, 2–3 in. (5–7.5 cm.) across, of very small funnel-shaped blooms; crimson or white; fragrant. Deadheading encourages a second, lesser flowering.
Season: Summer.
When to plant: Set transplants when available. Cold-hardy zone 3, heat-tolerant zone 9.
Light: Sunny to half-sunny.
Soil: Well drained, moist to on the dry side.
Fertilizer: 5-10-5.
Propagation: Divide established clumps or sow seeds in spring.
Uses: Beds, borders, pots, cut flowers.

CHRYSANTHEMUM
(kriss-ANTH-ee-mum)

Mum; Marguerite; Shasta, Painted, Oxeye, and Montauk Daisies

COMPOSITAE; daisy family

Height/habit: Low to high and shrubby; 1–6 ft. (30–180 cm.) high/wide.

Leaves: Entire, toothed, or pinnate, 1–3 in. (2.5–7.5 cm.) long/wide on stiff or woody stems; notably silver-edged in gold-and-silver mum (*C. pacificum*).

Flowers: Single or double "daisies" from less than 1 in. (2.5 cm.) across to 1 ft. (30 cm.); all colors except blue. Among species worth growing are the Shasta daisy (*C. maximum*); painted daisy, sometimes called pyrethrum (*C. coccineum*); oxeye daisy (*C. leucanthemum*); and Montauk daisy (*C. nipponicum*).

Season: Hardy garden mums (*C. morifolium*) of the North late summer until frost. These also bloom late spring through early summer in Southern gardens. Other species bloom variously spring through fall, zones 3–9. Marguerites (*C. frutescens*) bloom winter through spring in mild regions, through zone 10.

When to plant: Set transplants when available.

Light: Sunny to half-sunny.

Soil: Well drained, evenly moist.

Fertilizer: 5-10-5.

Propagation: Take cuttings or divide roots spring through early summer. Seeds of hardy garden mums started early indoors in late winter flower mid- to late fall.

Uses: Beds, borders, pots, cut flowers.

CIMICIFUGA
(simmy-SIFF-yew-gah)

Bugbane

RANUNCULACEAE; buttercup
family

Height/habit: High (3–8 ft.
[1–2.4 m.]) perennials native
to moist, shaded woodlands,
often seen gracing roadside
ditches from Connecticut to
Georgia and Tennessee.

Leaves: Cut into 3 parts, then
pinnate, 3–12 in. (7.5–30 cm.)
long/wide.

Flowers: Very small in panicles
to 2 ft. (61 cm.) long; some
species more wandlike than
others; white.

Season: Late summer through
fall.

When to plant: Set transplants
when available, ideally in
spring. Cold-hardy zones 3–4,
heat-tolerant zone 8.

Light: Half-shady to shady.

Soil: Well drained, humusy,
moist.

Fertilizer: 5-10-5.

Propagation: Sow seeds in
winter or divide roots of
established clumps in spring.

Uses: Back of beds and borders,
wild and woodland gardens,
at the shady edge of a pond.

CLEMATIS
(KLEHM-ah-tiss)

Clematis

RANUNCULACEAE; buttercup
family

Height/habit: Vining or semi-woody and climbing, 3–30 ft. (1–9 m.) high/wide. Exceptions are the bush types, such as *C. heracleifolia.*

Leaves: Compound, divided, often with tendril-forming tips; usually deciduous, though there are exceptions, such as evergreen *C. armandii.*

Flowers: Closed lanterns to open bells, 1–6 in. (2.5–15 cm.) across; some starry or doubled, others flattened; all colors, including blue.

Season: Spring through fall, depending on the clematis, for example: *C. alpina* cultivars typically bloom in spring; *C. montana rubens* early summer; *C. viticella* mid- to late summer; and *C. maximowicziana,* the popular sweet autumn clematis, early fall.

When to plant: Set transplants when available, rootstocks immediately on receipt from nursery. Clematis need a season to take hold. Cold- and heat-tolerant zones 3–9. Prune back in spring the old growth from clematis that bloom on the current season's shoots. Prune out in spring only the dead or straggly growth from any clematis to bloom on wood formed the previous season.

Light: Sunny to half-sunny for the clematis vine, shady for its roots.

Soil: Well drained, well dug, and enlivened by yearly top-dressing with well-rotted compost; add limestone as needed to afford the preferred "sweet," or alkaline, soil.

Fertilizer: 5-10-5.

Propagation: Layer, take stem cuttings, divide, or sow seeds in fall or spring.

Uses: Cover for fence, arbor, trellis, or tepee.

CLERODENDRUM
(klair-oh-DEN-drum)

Glory-bower

VERBENACEAE; verbena family

Height/habit: Bushes or twining vines to 15 ft. (4.5 m.) high/wide, but much smaller if grown in pots. The twiners, such as bleeding-heart vine (*C. thomsoniae*), are readily trained on a trellis or arbor and require only occasional pruning to remove dead wood and bloomed-out branches.
Leaves: Oval or heart-shaped, to 10 in. (25 cm.) long/wide, some giving off a pungent smell when disturbed.
Flowers: Showy heads to 6 in. (15 cm.) or more across; white, pink, rose, blue, or scarlet; *C. fragrans* notably fragrant.
Season: Summer through fall or winter through spring, depending on the climate and the species. *C. thomsoniae* is an outstanding summer performer outdoors, but it can also bloom indoors in winter.
When to plant: Set transplants when available. *C. bungei* colonizes well along the Gulf Coast. *C. thomsoniae, C. speciossissima*, and numerous other species are ground-hardy in zone 9; elsewhere they respond well to container culture, especially if placed outdoors in warm weather. *C. trichotomum*, whose fragrant white blooms appear mid- to late summer and are followed by showy blue berries, overwinters in the ground zones 6–7.
Light: Half-sunny to half-shady.
Soil: Humusy, well drained, moist.
Fertilizer: 14-14-14 timed-release or 30-10-10.
Propagation: Take root or stem cuttings in spring or summer.
Uses: Borders, pots, cover for trellis or arbor.

COREOPSIS
(koh-ree-OPP-siss)

Tickseed

COMPOSITAE; daisy family

Height/habit: Clumps 1–3 ft. (30–90 cm.) high/wide.
Leaves: Deeply cut and variable from the base of the plant to the flowering upper parts; 3–6 in. (7.5–15 cm.) long; very narrow in the thread-leaved *C. verticillata* and its offspring.
Flowers: Single or double daisies atop wiry, graceful stems; each flower 1–2 in. (2.5–5 cm.) across; all yellows, also pink in *C. rosea*. Deadheading is a boon to longer bloom life in many plants of this genus.
Season: Late spring through summer.
When to plant: Set transplants when available; sow seeds indoors 8–12 weeks before warm, planting-out weather for blooms the same season from newer hybrid strains. Widely cold- and heat-tolerant zones 3–10.
Light: Sunny to half-sunny.
Soil: Well drained, moist; tolerates drought after established.
Fertilizer: 5-10-5.
Propagation: Divide or sow seeds in spring or fall; alternatively, root airborne plantlets that form following bloom in some species.
Uses: Beds, borders, pots, cut flowers.

DELPHINIUM
(dell-FINN-ee-um)

Perennial Larkspur

RANUNCULACEAE; buttercup family

Height/habit: Among the garden's strongest vertical spire flowers, 3–8 ft. (1–2.4 m.). Staking required for all except the dwarfs.

Leaves: Deeply cut, most clustered in a clump at the base of the plant.

Flowers: Each to 2 in. (5 cm.) across, growing in florets, arranged all around the stems to several feet high. Prompt deadheading of the main spikes, followed by side-dressing the clumps with 5-10-5 fertilizer and watering, results in a bonus second flowering.

Season: Winter through spring in mild-winter regions, such as Southern California and along the Gulf Coast; summer zones 3–7.

When to plant: Set transplants when available, usually fall through winter in mild regions, spring elsewhere. Treat as annuals zones 8 and warmer, though they might possibly grow as perennials zones 3–7. However, they are rarely long-lived under the best of conditions in these zones.

Light: Sunny to half-sunny.

Soil: Well drained, moist.

Fertilizer: 5-10-5.

Propagation: Take cuttings of strong new shoots from the base of a particular variety in spring or sow fresh seeds late summer through early fall.

Uses: Beds, backs of borders, cut flowers.

DIANTHUS
(deye-ANTH-us)

Pink

CARYOPHYLLACEAE; pink family

Height/habit: Mat-forming, ground-hugging plants 3–8 in. (7.5–20 cm.) high/wide, with densely packed, spiky leaves are later smothered over the top with flowers, to 2–3 ft. (61–90 cm.) high/wide, some created for the cut-flower trade, others naturally higher, notably the yellow *D. knappii.*

Leaves: Narrow blades or grasslike, often blue-green or gray, to 2 in. (5 cm.) long.

Flowers: Single or double, to 3 in. (7.5 cm.) across, often laced or deeply cut at the edges; white, pink, rose, red, yellow, often bicolored; some clove-scented; *D. plumarius* is cottage pink. Deadheading encourages more blooms.

Season: Spring through summer.

When to plant: Set transplants when available. Perennials best zones 4–8. In warmer zones, especially those with high humidity, dianthus are sometimes set out as year-old transplants, for blooms that season as annuals.

Light: Sunny.

Soil: Well drained, moist to on the dry side.

Fertilizer: 5-10-5.

Propagation: Set stem cuttings to root in clean, sharp, moist sand in spring or summer.

Uses: Beds, borders, rock and wall gardens, pots, cut flowers.

DICENTRA
(deye-CENT-rah)

Bleeding Heart; Turkey Corn; Dutchman's breeches

FUMARIACEAE; fumitory family

Height/habit: Upright, arching clumps, 1–3 ft. (30–90 cm.) high/wide.
Leaves: Intricately cut and divided, 1–3 ft. (30–90 cm.).
Flowers: Nodding, heart- or pantaloon-shaped, each to 1 in. (2.5 cm.), on a graceful raceme; white, pink, rose, burgundy, or purple.

Season: Turkey corn (*D. eximia*) is attractive the longest time, spring through summer. Dutchman's-breeches (*D. cucullaria*) and bleeding heart (*D. spectabilis*) are for spring and early summer.
When to plant: Set transplants when available. Generally grown zones 3–9; the yellow-flowered, tendril-climbing *D. scandens* is for zones 6–9.
Light: Half-sunny to half-shady.
Soil: Humusy, well drained, moist.
Fertilizer: 5-10-5.
Propagation: Divide or sow seeds in fall (those self-sown often yield serendipitous results).
Uses: Beds; borders; rock, wall, and wild gardens; outdoor pots.

DICTAMNUS
(dick-TAM-nuss)

Gas Plant

RUTACEAE; rue family

Height/habit: Self-reliant, upright clumps, 2–4 ft. (61–122 cm.) high/wide.
Leaves: Glossy, lemon-scented, compound, 9–11 leaflets to 3 in. (7.5 cm.) long.
Flowers: To 1 in. (2.5 cm.) across in terminal clusters; white, pink, purplish rose.
Season: Early to midsummer. Leaves often die off by late summer, at which time they may be cut and removed to the compost pile.

When to plant: Set transplants when available. Long-lived in cold climates, best for zones 4–7.
Light: Sunny to partly shady.
Soil: Well drained, moist to on the dry side; tolerates drought after it is established.
Fertilizer: 5-10-5.
Propagation: Take root cuttings in spring or sow seeds in fall.
Uses: Beds, borders.

DIGITALIS
(dij-ih-TAY-liss)

Foxglove

SCROPHULARIACEAE; figwort family

Height/habit: First-year leaves in rosettes, to 1 ft. (30 cm.) high/wide. The second season a flower stalk rises from the center, 2–8 ft. (61–240 cm.) high.

Leaves: Hairy, gray-green, in a basal cluster.

Flowers: Tubular, as in the fingers of a glove; each flower 3 in. (7.5 cm.) long, growing on stalks 1–4 ft. (30–122 cm.) high; white, cream, yellow, pink, rose, or apricot. Prompt deadheading of the main spike results in a beautiful second flowering.

Season: Spring zones 9 and warmer; late spring through summer in cooler regions.

When to plant: Set transplants when available. Digitalis is at best a short-lived perennial, often treated as a biennial. Self-sows satisfactorily under favorable conditions and might even colonize a semiwild area.

Light: Half-sunny to shady.

Soil: Humusy, well drained, moist.

Fertilizer: 5-10-5.

Propagation: Divide roots in early fall or sow seeds in late summer.

Uses: Beds, borders, pots, cut flowers.

ECHINACEA
(eck-ih-NAY-see-ah)

Purple Coneflower

COMPOSITAE; daisy family

Height/habit: Upright to sprawling, 2–4 ft. (61–122 cm.) high/wide.

Leaves: Coarse ovals, mostly at the base, 2–6 in. (5–15 cm.) long.

Flowers: Single daisies 3–5 in. (7.5–12.5 cm.) across, with showy ray flowers surrounding a raised, brown-purple disk; white, pale to dark pink, rosy purple.

Season: Summer to fall.

When to plant: Set transplants when available or sow seeds at the beginning of a growing season, for blooms in a year or so. Cold-hardy zones 3–9.

Light: Sunny to half-sunny.

Soil: Well drained, moist to on the dry side; established plants tolerate drought.

Fertilizer: 5-10-5.

Propagation: Divide or sow seeds. The species *E. purpurea* and *E. pallida*, for example, are smaller and more graceful than the modern cultivars that are larger all around and more assertively upright.

Uses: Beds, borders, pots, cut flowers.

ECHINOPS
(ECK-ih-nopps)

Globe-thistle; Hedgehog Flower

COMPOSITAE; daisy family

Height/habit: Erect, to 5 ft. (1.5 m.) high by 2–3 ft. (61–90 cm.) wide.

Leaves: Coarse, thistlelike, 6–8 in. (15–20 cm.) long; variously spiny, set opposite along pale green to downy white stems.

Flowers: Round, spiny heads (echinops means "hedgehog-like"), 1–2 in. (2.5–5 cm.) across; blue, silvery blue, or white.

Season: Mid- to late summer.

When to plant: Set transplants when available, in clumps of 3 or more. Cold- and heat-tolerant zones 3–9.

Light: Sunny.

Soil: Well drained, moist to on the dry side. Tolerates drought when established.

Fertilizer: 5-10-5.

Propagation: Divide spring or fall or sow seeds for first blooms the second season.

Uses: Borders, backgrounds, large pots, cut flowers.

EPIMEDIUM
(eppy-MEE-dee-um)

Barrenwort

BERBERIDACEAE; barberry family

Height/habit: Spreading-upright, low-growing, 1–1.5 ft. (30–45 cm.) high/wide.
Leaves: Lance- to heart-shaped, 2–5 in. (5–12.5 cm.) long/wide; often burnished red in the spring; variously deciduous or evergreen in climates with mild winters.
Flowers: Delicate, airy, each 1–2 in. (2.5–5 cm.) across; white, violet, pink, red, yellow, purple, or orange, often with spur in contrasting color.

Season: Early to midspring.
When to plant: Set transplants when available. Variously cold-tolerant zones 3–5; heat-tolerant through zone 9.
Light: Half-sunny to half-shady.
Soil: Humusy, well drained, moist.
Fertilizer: 5-10-5.
Propagation: Divide in spring or fall.
Uses: Beds, borders, rock gardens, shady wild gardens, ground cover.

ERYNGIUM
(uhr-IN-jee-um)

Sea Holly

UMBELLIFERAE; parsley or carrot family

Height/habit: Upright to sprawling, 1–4 ft. (30–122 cm.) high by half as wide.
Leaves: Spiny, thistlelike, 6–12 in. (15–30 cm.) long; often heart-shaped at the base, lobed or hand-shaped up toward the flowering parts; green to blue-gray, some with showy white veining.
Flowers: Resemble thistles; 1-in.- (2.5-cm.-) wide cones surrounded by 2–4-in.- (5–10-cm.-) wide bracts; blue to steel-blue and silvery.

Season: Mid- to late summer.
When to plant: Set transplants when available. Cold- and heat-tolerant zones 4–8.
Light: Sunny.
Soil: Well drained, moist to on the dry side.
Fertilizer: 5-10-5.
Propagation: Sow seed in spring or take root cuttings in late winter.
Uses: Borders, cottage gardens, cutting for dried bouquets.

EUPATORIUM
(yew-pah-TOH-ree-um)

Boneset;
Mist Flower;
Hardy Ageratum;
Joe-pye Weed;
White Snakeroot

COMPOSITAE; daisy family

Height/habit: Upright bushes, 2–3 ft. (61–90 cm.); hardy ageratum, or mist flower (*E. coelstinum*), 3–4 ft. (1–1.2 m.); white snakeroot (*E. rugosum*), 8–10 ft. (2.4–3 m.); joe-pye weed (*E. fistulosum*), 6–10 ft. (1.8–3 m.) by half as wide.

Leaves: Lance-shaped, 3–12 in. (7.5–30 cm.) long; opposite or whorled, coarse texture.

Flowers: Fuzzy, growing in rounded or flat-topped clusters, 4–6 in. (10–15 cm.) across, over the tops of the plants; white, blue-violet, red-violet, pinkish lavender.

Season: Late summer through fall.

When to plant: Set transplants when available. Cold-tolerant zones 2–3, heat-tolerant zones 8–9.

Light: Sunny to half-shady.

Soil: Humusy, well drained, moist. Tolerates drought when established.

Fertilizer: 5-10-5.

Propagation: Divide in spring.

Uses: Borders; cottage, meadow, butterfly, and wild gardens; cut flowers; ageratum also for pots.

EUPHORBIA
(yew-FOR-bee-ah)
Cypress Spurge
EUPHORBIACEAE; spurge family

Height/habit: *E. cyparissias*
upright to sprawling or spreading, 1–6 ft. (30–180 cm.)
high/wide.

Leaves: Narrow, lance- to
spear-shaped, in the manner
of some long-needled conifers;
1–4 in. (2–10 cm.) long.

Flowers: Inconspicuous in
terminal clusters, surrounded
by yellowish green bracts,
2–4 in. (5–10 cm.) across, that
scintillate in the sun.

Season: Spring through early
summer.

When to plant: Set transplants
when available. Variously cold-
hardy zones 3–8; heat-tolerant
zone 9, but not successful
with heat and high humidity
together. The genus contains
thousands of species, some
weeds, some ornamentals
adapted to nearly every climate
and garden.

Light: Sunny to half-shady.

Soil: Well drained, moist to
on the dry side; some very
drought-tolerant when
established.

Fertilizer: 5-10-5.

Propagation: Divide in spring,
taking care not to harm the
roots. Or sow seed in late
winter through early spring.

Uses: Beds, borders, rock
gardens, pots.

GAURA
(GARR-ah)

Wild Honeysuckle

ONAGRACEAE; evening-primrose family

Height/habit: Bushy and upright to sprawling, 2–4 ft. (61–122 cm.) high/wide.
Leaves: Lance-shaped, to 3 in. (7.5 cm.) long, mostly toward the base of the plant.
Flowers: Each to 1 in. (2.5 cm.) across, growing mothlike on long, wiry stems; white changing to pink in a day, then disappearing. Cutting back flowered-out stalks encourages more blooms.

Season: Summer through fall.
When to plant: Set transplants when available. Cold- and heat-tolerant zones 6–9; better suited to drier climates than those likely to be humid and hot at the same time.
Light: Sunny.
Soil: Well drained, moist to on the dry side. Tolerates drought when established.
Fertilizer: 5-10-5.
Propagation: Sow seeds in spring. Allow several years for a gaura plant to hit its stride.
Uses: Beds, borders, pots, Xeriscape.

GERANIUM
(juh-RAY-nee-um)

Cranesbill

GERANIACEAE; geranium family

Height/habit: Bushy and upright to trailing/sprawling, 4–24 in. (10–61 cm.) high/wide. Staking or brushing helpful for the higher species.

Leaves: Many-lobed, often toothed and hairy, some evergreen.

Flowers: 5-petaled, saucer-shaped, 1–2 in. (2.5–5 cm.) across; white, pink, rose, violet, blue, purple, often with veining in a contrasting color. Shearing after first flowering encourages a second bloom. Also grown for beaklike seed heads.

Season: Spring, summer, or fall, some in 2 seasons.

When to plant: Set transplants when available. Variously cold-hardy zones 4–5, heat-tolerant zones 8–9.

Light: Sunny to shady, depending on the species and the local conditions; the hotter the summer the more shade.

Soil: Humusy, well drained, moist.

Fertilizer: 5-10-5.

Propagation: Divide or take stem and root cuttings in spring or early fall. Sow seeds in winter for blooms in 2 years.

Uses: Beds, borders, pots, wild and rock gardens.

HELIOPSIS
(hee-lee-OPP-siss)

Oxeye

COMPOSITAE; daisy family

Height/habit: Upright, 3–5 ft. (1–1.5 m.) high/wide. Brush staking as shoots emerge in spring results in self-reliant high plants later on.
Leaves: Coarsely toothed, rounded lance- to egg-shaped, to 5 in. (12.5 cm.) long.
Flowers: Big, brassy single or semidouble daisies, 2–4 in. (5–10 cm.) across; saturated yellow or golden-orange. Deadheading increases bloom and creates a tidy appearance.
Season: Summer into fall.

When to plant: Set transplants when available. Cold- and heat-tolerant zones 4–9.
Light: Sunny.
Soil: Well drained, moist to on the dry side.
Fertilizer: 5-10-5.
Propagation: Divide in spring or fall or sow seeds winter through spring; some cultivars come true from seeds and may flower by the end of their first season.
Uses: Beds, borders (usually in middle or toward the back), large pots, cut flowers.

HELLEBORUS
(hell-lebb-OH-russ)

Christmas Rose; Lenten Rose; Stinking Hellebore

RANUNCULACEAE; buttercup family

Height/habit: Fairly tidy, compact mounds, 1–1.5 ft. (30–45 cm.) high/wide.
Leaves: Palm-shaped, deeply divided, 8–16 in. (20–40 cm.) across, lasting through winter until removed to make way for flowering and new foliage.
Flowers: Nodding bells or cups, 2–4 in. (5–10 cm.) across; white, pink, rose, purple, green.

Season: Winter through spring.
When to plant: Set transplants when available, usually spring. Christmas rose (*H. niger*) and stinking hellebore (*H. foetidus*) generally cold- and heat-tolerant zones 3–9; Lenten rose (*H. orientalis*) zones 5–9.
Light: Half-sunny to shady. The hotter the climate, the more shade helleborus needs.
Soil: Humusy, well drained, moist.
Fertilizer: 5-10-5.
Propagation: Divide or transplant self-sown seedlings in spring.
Uses: Outstanding for shade and wild gardens; also beds, borders, cut flowers.

HEMEROCALLIS
(hem-er-oh-KAY-liss)

Daylily

LILIACEAE; lily family

Height/habit: Grassy clumps, 1–4 ft. (30–122 cm.) high/wide.
Leaves: V-shaped, long, narrow, grasslike, each 1–2 ft. (30–61 cm.) long; deciduous types better in cold-winter regions, evergreen varieties in the South.
Flowers: Single or double, saucers or trumpets, some spidery, 2–8 in. (5–20 cm.) across; all colors except blue. Some are fragrant. Dead-heading does not prolong bloom but it is a morning ritual for most serious daylily growers.

Season: Midspring to early fall. Some daylilies bloom only once a year, but the breeding trend is toward repeat bloomers and even toward those that bloom intermittently over a protracted season. It is the nature of the daylily to open a flower in the morning and close it forever at the end of that day. Modern hybrids may open the evening before and remain into the evening of the following day, or even stay open for two days.
When to plant: Set transplants when available. Daylilies are often sold in pots or right in the field where they can be selected, dug, and moved while in bloom. Cold- and heat-tolerant zones 3–9.
Light: Sunny to half-sunny. Too much shade reduces or rules out bloom in daylilies.

Soil: Well drained, moist to on the dry side. Tolerates drought when established, especially so when not actively budding and blooming.
Fertilizer: 5-10-5.
Propagation: Divide in early spring or immediately following bloom. Seeds started in the spring may give some bloom in the second season.
Uses: Beds, borders, miniatures in pots, ground cover.

HEUCHERA
(HEW-kur-ah)

Coralbells;
Alumroot

SAXIFRAGACEAE; saxifrage family

Height/habit: Low, mounding
plants, 1–3 ft. (30–90 cm.)
high/wide, often with the main
mass of foliage concentrated
at the lower third of the total
height.

Leaves: Rounded to heart-
shaped, lobed and scalloped,
often toothed; 1–6 in.
(2.5–15 cm.) in diameter;
usually dark evergreen, except
notably dark purple in
H. micrantha 'Palace Purple'
and purple-veined in alumroot
(*H. americana* 'Sunset').

Flowers: Tiny, growing in
panicles that are 6–12 in.
(15–30 cm.) long, carried well
above the foliage mass on
graceful, hairy stems; white,
pink, rose, red, or scarlet.
Remove the flowering stems
when bloom finishes to
play up the tidy aspects of
the heuchera plant.

Season: Late spring through
early summer, except hairy
alumroot (*H. villosa*) in late
summer through fall.

When to plant: Set transplants
when available. Cold- and heat-
tolerant zones 4–9.

Light: Sun to half shade; the
hotter the climate, the greater
heuchera's need for shade in
summer.

Soil: Humusy, well drained,
moist.

Fertilizer: 5-10-5.

Propagation: Divide in spring
or fall. Sow seeds in spring
for nice-sized transplants the
following year and blooms
the next.

Uses: Beds; borders; pots;
shade, rock, and wild gardens.

HOSTA
(HOSS-tah)
Plaintain Lily
LILIACEAE; lily family

Height/habit: Upright, arching clumps or curving mounds, 1–3 ft. (30–90 cm.) high and as wide or wider, with flowers in season rising above.

Leaves: Varying from narrow lance or linear shapes to broad hearts with elegant vein quilting, from 6–12 in. (15–30 cm.) long/wide; all greens, from chartreuse to bluish, also gold and silvery white, in endless variations. Slugs and snails are a perennial problem. Treat as necessary to maintain healthy leaves.

Flowers: Funnel-shaped, 1–3 in. (2.5–7.5 cm.) long; white, pale to violet-blue or lavender; some fragrant, notably *H. plantaginea.* Some growers of the more highly variegated hostas prefer to remove the flowering stalks before they bloom.

Season: Spring until fall for foliage. Late spring through early summer until early fall for flowers—the season depending on the variety. Almost all year in mildest regions, although long, hot, humid summers are not beneficial.

When to plant: Set transplants when available. Often sold in nursery pots fully grown, even in bloom, so that it's possible to create instant effects. Cold- and heat-tolerant zones 3–9.

Light: Sunny in cooler climates to shady in the hottest.

Soil: Humusy, well drained, moist. Surprisingly drought-tolerant when established.

Fertilizer: 14-14-14 timed-release; or side-dress with well-rotted compost.

Propagation: Divide in spring or fall. Hostas can be subdivided fairly rapidly to plant an area with ground cover, but it is also true that they grow best if left undisturbed.

Uses: Beds, borders, pots, wild and shade gardens; leaves and flowers for arranging.

HOUTTUYNIA
(who-TEN-ee-ah)

Houttuynia

SAURURACEAE; lizard's-tail family

Height/habit: Spreading ground cover, 6–18 in. (15–45 cm.) high/wide.
Leaves: Heart-shaped, to 3 in. (7.5 cm.) long/wide; when crushed, yield odor that is unpleasant to some; variegated white, cream, red, and green in the cultivar *H. cordata* 'Chameleon,' also known as 'Variegata.'
Flowers: 2-in. (5-cm.) spikes, inconspicuous, somewhat showier in the double white *H. cordata* 'Flore Pleno.'
Season: Foliage variously attractive depending on the season and the climate, usually midspring through summer.

Grown in the right place, this plant can be quite successful (especially the variegated and the double-flowered types).
When to plant: Set transplants when available. Cold- and heat-tolerant zones 6-9.
Light: Sunny to part shady. Most compact in cooler climate and full sun.
Soil: Humusy, well drained, moist to wet.
Fertilizer: 14-14-14 timed-release.
Propagation: Divide or take cuttings in spring or summer.
Uses: Ground cover for a wet place (can spread to the point of being invasive), pots.

INULA
(INN-yew-lah)

Elecampane

COMPOSITAE; daisy family

Height/habit: Upright or sprawling, reaching 2–6 ft. (61–180 cm.), with masses of coarse leaves toward the base, crowned in season by green-collared and often showy golden daisies.
Leaves: Oblong to elliptical, 6 in. (15 cm.) long, as in *I. hookeri*, to 2 ft. (61 cm.) long, as in *I. helenium*; clustered toward the base, often thinning or disappearing entirely from the flowering stalks.
Flowers: Single daisies, 2–6 in. (5–15 cm.) across; all yellows, from pale to dark; very responsive to deadheading.

Season: Summer through fall.
When to plant: Set transplants when available. Sword-leaf inula (*I. ensifolia*) and *I. helenium* cold- and heat-tolerant zones 3–9; other species zones 4–8, excepting Himalayan elecampane (*I. royleana*), suited only to the cooler zones 3–7.
Light: Sunny.
Soil: Well drained, moist.
Fertilizer: 5-10-5.
Propagation: Divide in spring or fall or sow seeds in spring.
Uses: Beds, borders, wild and meadow gardens, large pots, cut flowers.

IPOMOPSIS
(ipp-oh-MOPP-siss)
Standing Cypress
POLEMONIACEAE; phlox family

Height/habit: Slender, leafy stalks crowned by torches of flowers reaching 4–6 ft. (1.2–1.8 m.).

Leaves: Finely dissected, 4–6 in. (10–15 cm.) long/wide, growing in a basal rosette the first year, on strongly vertical stems in the second.

Flowers: Tubular, each to 1 in. (2.5 cm.) long, blooming in profusion; orange-red or apricot.

Season: Summer: early in hot climates, later in cool.

When to plant: Set transplants when available. Seedlings started the first year bloom the next and die. Colonizes readily in the right site and performs as a self-reliant perennial.

Light: Sunny.

Soil: Well drained, moist to on the dry side.

Fertilizer: 5-10-5.

Propagation: Sow seeds in spring or summer.

Uses: Beds, borders, pots, wild and meadow gardens, Xeriscape.

IRIS
(EYE-riss)

Flag; Fleur-de-lis

IRIDACEAE; iris family

Height/habit: Upright, tidy fountains of grassy leaves in the highly rated Siberian iris (*I. sibirica*), 2–4 ft. (61–122 cm.) high, nearly as wide; short, perky fans in the native woodland dwarf crested iris (*I. cristata*), 6–9 in. (15–22.5 cm.) high/wide; evergreen clumps to 2 ft. (61 cm.) high/wide in the unfortunately named stinking iris (*I. foetidissima*); leaves odorous when crushed but pale violet flowers are followed by long-lasting, showy red berries.

Leaves: Swordlike or similar to blades of grass, 9–30 in. (22.5–76 cm.) long, mostly 1 in. (2.5 cm.) wide or less; bluish to dark green, some evergreen.

Flowers: Fleur-de-lis-shaped, 2–5 in. (5–12.5 cm.) across; most colors; some fragrant.

Season: Spring through early summer.

When to plant: Set transplants when available. Siberian iris rated cold- and heat-tolerant zones 3–9 ('Caesar's Brother' performs well along the Gulf Coast); *I. foetidissima* is for zones 7–9; *I. cristata* zones 4–8.

Light: Sunny, except part to full shade for *I. cristata*.

Soil: Well drained, moist; on the dry side acceptable after flowering, when established.

Fertilizer: 5-10-5.

Propagation: Divide in early spring or late summer.

Uses: Beds, borders, ground covers, pots.

JASMINUM
(JAZZ-min-um)

Jasmine

OLEACEAE; olive family

Height/habit: Twining or shrubby vines, 5–30 ft. (1.5–9 m.) high/wide.
Leaves: Simple or pinnate, 3–6 in. (7.5–15 cm.) long, often glossy and evergreen. *J. nudiflorum* deciduous and flowers (yellow) while leafless.
Flowers: Borne singly or in clusters, each 1–2 in. (2.5–5 cm.) across; slender tube flaring into corolla with 4–9 lobes; there are also doubles and hose-in-hose types; white or yellow; usually fragrant.
Season: Almost any time of year, depending on the kind of jasmine and weather conditions. *J. polyanthum* blooms white blushed with pink in mild-climate winter through spring, in gardens or cool greenhouses. 'Maid of Orleans' blooms all year, especially well through warm weather. *J. tortuosum* blooms with starry white flowers all year and will quickly cover a trellis or lace over and around an arbor.
When to plant: Set transplants when available. *J. nudiflorum* cold-hardy zones 6–7, heat-tolerant zones 8–9. Grow tropical and subtropical species in pots or outdoors zones 8–9 and warmer.
Light: Sunny to half-sunny.
Soil: Humusy, well drained, moist.
Fertilizer: 5-10-5.
Propagation: Take cuttings of half-mature wood in spring or summer.
Uses: Cover for trellis, arbor, or tepee.

JUSTICIA
(juss-TIH-see-ah)

Shrimp Plant; King's Crown

ACANTHACEAE; acanthus family

Height/habit: Upright, branching tropical American shrubs, 3–5 (1–1.5 m.) ft. high, capable of spreading to similar width.
Leaves: Oval, hairy, 2–12 in. (5–30 cm.) long and nearly as wide, often with prominent midveins, in opposite pairs along square stems. Foliage can also be boldly textured for interesting contrast.
Flowers: Showy clusters, so dense on shrimp plant (*J. brandegeana*) that its leaves are hidden by bracts of salmon pink, chartreuse, or lemon yellow; appearing as a plume of feathery pink or white at top of king's crown (*J. carnea* and varieties); in yellow king's crown (*J. aurea*), flowers yellow and larger.

Season: Primarily warm-weather plants. Shrimp plant can bloom all year in mild-climate gardens, making an unexpected show at midspring.
When to plant: Set transplants when available. Freshly rooted cuttings form the best flowering plants each new season. Container and bedding plants zones 8 and colder. Zones 9 and warmer they live in the garden through winter, surviving from the roots in all but exceptionally cold years.
Light: Sunny to half-shady; more shade in the hotter climates.
Soil: Humusy, well drained, moist throughout the active growing season.
Fertilizer: 14-14-14 timed-release, 5-10-5 at flowering.
Propagation: Take stem cuttings in spring or summer.
Uses: Pots, beds, borders, cottage gardens.

LAMIUM
(LAY-mee-um)

Dead Nettle

LABIATAE; mint family

Height/habit: Trailing plants to 2 ft. (61 cm.), sprawling in *L. galeobdolon* (yellow flowers), tidier in *L. maculatum* and its cultivated forms, 1–1.5 ft. (30–45 cm.) high/wide.
Leaves: Simple, toothed, set opposite along square stems; often variegated paler green, silvery, or yellow.
Flowers: To 1 in. (2.5 cm.) across, in whorls at the upper leaf axils; white, yellow, pink, or purple.
Season: Flowers late spring through summer. However, light shearing after flowering concentrates energy on the foliage, an important part of lamium's appeal.
When to plant: Set transplants when available.
Light: Half-sunny to half-shady.
Soil: Humusy, well drained, moist.
Fertilizer: 14-14-14 timed-release at the time of planting, possibly 5-10-5 at start of next flowering season.
Propagation: Take stem cuttings spring through early summer; divide spring or fall.
Uses: Ground cover under trees and shrubs, shade or wild gardens, pots.

LAVANDULA
(lah-VAN-dew-lah)

Lavender

LABIATAE; mint family

Height/habit: Small shrubs, 1–3 ft. (30–90 cm.) high/wide.

Leaves: Narrow and spiky or broader and cut fernlike, 1–2 in. (2.5–5 cm.) long; grayish to blue-green.

Flowers: Very small in packed spikes, 1–3 in. (2.5–7.5 cm.) long, growing above the foliage; English lavender (*L. officinalis*) is true lavender color. French lavender (*L. stoechas*) has showy purple bracts.

Season: Spring and again in fall if cut back after blooming; year-round in mild climates.

When to plant: Set transplants when available. English lavender is hardly a stranger to most gardeners, yet its cold and heat tolerance as a garden plant is through zones 7–8—perhaps 9 if the climate is dry. The other lavenders are grown outdoors all year zones 8–10, elsewhere in pots brought indoors at the threat of freezing weather.

Light: Sunny.

Soil: Well drained, moist to on the dry side. Tolerates drought when established.

Fertilizer: 5-10-5.

Propagation: Divide in early spring; sow seeds in spring through summer, especially those of *L. officinalis* 'Lady,' an All-America Selections winner that blooms the first year; take stem cuttings late summer through early fall.

Uses: Beds, borders, pots, hedging, cutting fresh or dried.

LIATRIS
(leye-YAY-triss)

Gay-feather

COMPOSITAE; daisy family

Height/habit: 2–6 ft. (61–180 cm.) high and half as wide.

Leaves: Narrow, linear leaves, 6–12 in. (15–30 cm.) long, appear first in a clump, then become gradually smaller and grow farther apart as main stem shoots up.

Flowers: Straight, dense spikes, 6–12 in. (15–30 cm.) long, flowering from the top of the plant down; reddish purple or white.

Season: Late summer through early fall zones 7 and colder; often late spring through early summer in warmer zones.

When to plant: Set transplants when available. Cold-hardy zone 4; heat-tolerant through zone 9 if arid, zone 8 if moist.

Light: Sunny.

Soil: Well drained, moist to on the dry side. Tolerates drought when established.

Fertilizer: 5-10-5.

Propagation: Sow seeds or divide in early spring.

Uses: Beds, borders, wild gardens, pots, cut flowers.

LIGULARIA
(ligg-yew-LAY-ree-ah)

Leopard Plant; Silver Farfugium

COMPOSITAE; daisy family

Height/habit: Choice foliage plants 2–4 ft. (61–122 cm.) high by nearly as wide. *L. przewalskii* (possibly a hybrid with *L. stenocephala*) 'The Rocket' is an example of one with spectacular flowers as well.

Leaves: Rounded hearts, kidney shapes, or toothed lobes, 1–2 ft. (30–61 cm.) across; besides green, they can be purple, as in *L. dentata* ('Desdemona'), spotted and splashed with yellow in leopard plant (*L. tussilaginea* 'Aureo-maculata'), or edged and variegated white in silver farfugium (*L. t.* 'Argentea').

Flowers: Small "daisies" massed dramatically in the 4-ft. (1.2-m.) spires produced by 'The Rocket'; gardeners often remove the buds from leopard plant and silver farfugium since actual flowering detracts from the leaves.

Season: Mid- to late summer for flowers; foliage attractive most seasons.

When to plant: Set transplants when available. Cold- and heat-tolerant zones 4–8, except zones 8 and warmer for leopard plant and silver farfugium.

Light: Half-sunny for flowering types ('The Rocket'), mostly shade for foliage types.

Soil: Humusy, moist to wet.

Fertilizer: 14-14-14 timed-release when planting, 5-10-5 later only to encourage bloom.

Propagation: Divide in spring.

Uses: Bold feature in a wet site with afternoon shade. Leopard plant and silver farfugium do well in large pots in shade.

LOBELIA
(loh-BEE-lee-ah)

Cardinal Flower; Great Blue Lobelia

LOBELIACEAE; lobelia family

Height/habit: Tidy basal rosettes rise into slender flowering columns, 4–6 ft. (1.2–1.8 m.) high by 1 ft. (30 cm.) wide.

Leaves: Egg- to lance-shaped, 4–6 in. (10–15 cm.) long; some have reddish purple foliage and stems.

Flowers: Prominently 3-lobed at the bottom and distinctly spiky at the top, 1–2 in. (2.5–5 cm.) across, in many-flowered spikes; red in cardinal flower (*L. cardinalis*), light blue in great blue lobelia (*L. siphilitica*). Permit seed heads to develop, in the interest of fostering self-sown seedlings.

Season: Mid- to late summer, early fall.

When to plant: Set transplants when available. Cardinal flower cold- and heat-tolerant zones 2–9; great blue lobelia, zones 4–8.

Light: Half-sunny to shady.

Soil: Humusy, well drained, moist to wet.

Fertilizer: 5-10-5.

Propagation: Divide or sow seeds in spring; divide or take stem cuttings midsummer.

Uses: Beds, borders, streamside, wild and meadow gardens, pots, cut flowers.

LONICERA
(lonn-ISS-er-ah)

Honeysuckle

CAPRIFOLIACEAE; honeysuckle family

Height/habit: Shrubs or vines, from 3 to 80 ft. (1-24 m.) high/wide.

Leaves: Opposite pairs, 1–2 in. (2.5–5 cm.) long; joined together at the base so as to appear they are one with the flowering stem passing through; some blue-green, also evergreen.

Flowers: Tubular, 1–6 in. (2.5–15 cm.), in clusters; white, yellow, pink, purple, rose, or red; some of the most fragrant are *L. fragrantissima*, *L. hildebrandtiana*, *L. japonica*, *L. nitida*, *L. periclymenum* (especially in the variety 'Belgica'), and *L. pileata*.

Season: Spring to fall, some everblooming.

When to plant: Set transplants when available. There are locally adapted varieties having fragrant flowers and acceptable garden manners for almost every cold and heat zone. Zones 5–9 *L. fragrantissima* and *L. periclymenum*; 4–9 *L. japonica*; zone 9 *L. hildebrandtiana*.

Light: Sunny to half-sunny.

Soil: Well drained, moist to on the dry side.

Fertilizer: 5-10-5.

Propagation: Take stem cuttings or layer spring or summer.

Uses: Ground cover; cover for trellis, arbor, or fence; shrubbery border; wild and cottage gardens; cut flowers.

LUPINUS
(loo-PEYE-nus)

Lupine; Texas Bluebonnet

LEGUMINOSAE; pea family

Height/habit: Concentrated clumps, 1–2 ft. (30–61 cm.) high/wide.

Leaves: Fingerlike leaflets, 6–12 in. (15–30 cm.) long, silky-hairy in some.

Flowers: Similar to those of butterfly pea, to 1 in. (2.5 cm.) across, densely and orderly packed along high spikes, 1–2 ft. (30–61 cm.) long; all colors, many bicolors, strong in pastels, clear blues, oranges, and pinks.

Season: Spring through summer.

When to plant: Set transplants when available. Cold- and heat-tolerant zones 4–7, although not by nature long-lived under the best of conditions. Often treated as spring-flowering annuals, zones 8–9.

Light: Sunny.

Soil: Well drained, moist to on the dry side.

Fertilizer: 5-10-5.

Propagation: Sow seeds winter through spring; divide roots carefully in early spring.

Uses: Beds, borders, large pots, wild and meadow gardens, cut flowers.

LYCHNIS
(LISH-niss; LIKE-niss)

Campion

CARYOPHYLLACEAE; pink family

Height/habit: Clump-forming or trailing, 1.5–4 ft. (45–122 cm.) high/wide.
Leaves: Egg-, linear-, or lance-shaped, to 6 in. (15 cm.) long; woolly gray in *L. coronaria* and *L. flos-jovis*.
Flowers: Borne singly or clustered, each 1–2 in. (2.5–5 cm.) across; red scarlet, pink, white, rose, magenta, or orange.
Season: Summer.

When to plant: Set transplants when available. Cold- and heat-tolerant zones 4–8, 9 if not too hot and humid.
Light: Sunny to partly sunny.
Soil: Well drained, moist.
Fertilizer: 5-10-5.
Propagation: Divide in spring or fall; alternatively, take basal cuttings in spring or sow seeds in late spring.
Uses: Beds, borders, pots, cut flowers; cottage, wild, or meadow gardens.

LYSIMACHIA
(leye-sim-ACK-ee-ah)

Loosestrife;
Creeping Jennie

PRIMULACEAE; primrose family

Height/habit: Trailing in creeping Jennie (*L. nummularia*) and *L. procumbens*, to 8 in. (20 cm.) high x 2 ft. (61 cm.) wide; upright in gooseneck loosestrife (*L. clethroides*) and the yellow *L. punctata*, 2–3 ft. (61–90 cm.) high by half as wide.

Leaves: Egg- to spear-shaped, 4–6 in. (10–15 cm.) long.

Flowers: Very small but showy in dense spires or open spikes; white or yellow. *L. procumbens* larger, to 1 in. (2.5 cm.) across, yellow, in terminal clusters.

Season: Mostly spring for *L. procumbens*; summer for creeping Jennie and gooseneck and yellow loosestrife.

When to plant: Set transplants when available. Cold- and heat-tolerant zones 3–4 to zones 8–9, except *L. procumbens*, zones 8–9, well-suited to container gardening in cold climates.

Light: Sunny to partly shady.

Soil: Humusy, well drained, moist.

Fertilizer: 5-10-5.

Propagation: Divide or take stem cuttings spring or fall.

Uses: Beds, borders, pots, cut flowers; wild and bog gardens. Inclined to being invasive; beautiful when well managed. Creeping Jennie used primarily for foliage effect as a ground cover or spilling from a hanging basket.

MALVA
(MAL-vah)
Mallow
MALVACEAE; mallow family

Height/habit: Upright, 2–4 ft. (61–122 cm.) high/wide.
Leaves: Lobed or dissected, 6–12 in. (15–30 cm.) across.
Flowers: Distinctively lobed and notched, 1–2 in. (2.5–5 cm.) across; white to rose pink and lavender with purple veins.
Season: Late spring through fall.
When to plant: Set transplants when available. Cold- and heat-tolerant zones 3–4 to 8–9.
Light: Sunny in cooler climates to half-shady in warmer.
Soil: Well drained, moist.
Fertilizer: 5-10-5.
Propagation: Divide in spring or fall; take cuttings of basal shoots in spring.
Uses: Beds, borders, cottage and wild gardens, pots.

MACLEAYA
(mack-LAY-ah)
Plume Poppy
PAPAVERACEAE; poppy family

Height/habit: Upright clumps, 8–10 ft. (2.4–3 m.) high by half as wide. May require staking.
Leaves: Heart-shaped, lobed, to 8 in. (20 cm.) across, undersides covered with white felt.
Flowers: Petals absent, in plumes to 1 ft. (30 cm.) long; creamy, white, buff, or pink (in *M. cordata* 'Flamingo').
Season: Summer until fall.
When to plant: Set transplants when available. Cold- and heat-tolerant zones 4–9.
Light: Sunny to half-sunny.
Soil: Humusy, well drained, moist.
Fertilizer: 5-10-5.
Propagation: Divide in spring or fall; take cuttings of basal shoots in spring.
Uses: Accent, back of border, wild garden. Can be invasive.

MANDEVILLA
(man-duh-VILL-ah)

Mandeville; Chilean Jasmine

APOCYNACEAE; dogbane family

Height/habit: Twining, flowering vines, 5–30 ft. (1.5–9 m.).

Leaves: Elliptic to oblong, 2–6 in. (5–15 cm.) long.

Flowers: Showy funnelforms, 2–4 in. (5–10 cm.) across the face; white, pink, cherry red, or yellow; fragrant in white Chilean jasmine (*M. laxa*).

Season: During warm, frost-free weather, which can include winter in a cold-climate greenhouse. Well-grown mandevillas often bloom through 3 seasons.

When to plant: Set transplants when available. Cold-hardy zone 10; elsewhere grow as container plants that can be brought to a warm place when outdoor temperatures drop below 50°F (10°C).

Light: Sunny to half-sunny.

Soil: Humusy, well drained, moist.

Fertilizer: 14-14-14 timed-release; 5-10-5 at flowering time.

Propagation: Take stem cuttings in spring or summer.

Uses: Cover for trellis, fence, or tepee.

MISCANTHUS
(mis-KAN-thus)

Eulalia; Japanese Silver Grass

GRAMINEAE; grass family

Height/habit: Mostly upright and clump-forming, plumes rise above foliage 8–12 ft. (2.4–3.6 m.).

Leaves: Grasslike, arching, 1–2 in. (2.5–5 cm.) across; 6 in. (15 cm.) to 6 ft. (1.8 m.) long.

Flowers: Panicles or plumes, 10–15 in. (25–38 cm.) long; silvery, pale pink to red.

Season: For foliage effect almost all year. Flowers summer through fall.

When to plant: Set transplants when available. Widely and locally adapted, zones 5–9.

Light: Sunny to half-sunny.

Soil: Well drained, moist to on the dry side.

Fertilizer: 5-10-5 or 14-14-14 timed-release.

Propagation: Divide in spring. Most grasses need cutting back in early spring to clear the way for fresh new blades. Leave them standing through winter, however, for visual interest, to catch snow, and as wildlife shelter.

Uses: Beds; borders; pots; background plantings; Xeriscape; cottage, meadow, and wild gardens; seed heads for dried arrangements.

MONARDA
(mohn-ARD-ah)

Bee Balm; Oswego Tea

LABIATAE; mint family

Height/habit: *M. didyma* in upright to sprawling clumps, 2–4 ft. (61–122 cm.) high/wide.
Leaves: Egg-shaped, toothed and pointed, 3–6 in. (7.5–15 cm.) long; scented.
Flowers: Tubular, to 1 in. (2.5 cm.) long, in dense, whorled clusters; white, pink, red, lavender, or purple.

Season: Summer.
When to plant: Set transplants when available.
Light: Sunny to half-sunny.
Soil: Humusy, well drained, moist to wet. Dryness aids mildew.
Fertilizer: 5-10-5.
Propagation: Divide in spring.
Uses: Beds, borders, streamside, pots, wild and bog gardens, cut flowers. Attractive to bees, butterflies, and hummingbirds.

NEPETA
(NEPP-ett-ah)

Catmint

LABIATAE; mint family

Height/habit: Clump, mound, or bushy upright, 1–3 ft. (30–90 cm.) high/wide.
Leaves: Egg-shaped, softly toothed, to 1 in. (2.5 cm.) long.
Flowers: To 1 in. (2.5 cm.) in plentiful spikes; white, bluish lavender, or pale yellow.
Season: Summer.
When to plant: Set transplants when available. Cold- and heat-tolerant zones 3–4 to 8–9. Pale yellow *N. govaniana* is least tolerant of hot summers. *N. x faassenii* and cultivars 'Dropmore' and 'Six Hills Giant' best general garden plants.
Light: Sunny to partly shady.
Soil: Well drained, moist.
Fertilizer: 5-10-5.
Propagation: Divide in spring or take cuttings in summer.
Uses: Beds, borders, ground cover, pots.

NEPHROLEPIS
(nee-FROLL-e-pis)

Sword Fern; Boston Fern

POLYPODIACEAE; polypody family

Height/habit: Tidy clumps or in self-reliant colonies, 1–3 ft. (30–90 cm.) high/wide.
Leaves: Narrow arching or drooping fronds, 1–3 ft. (30–90 cm.) long; sometimes feathery in Boston fern (*N. exaltata* var. *bostoniensis*).
Season: Spring through fall; all year zone 10.
When to plant: Set transplants when available.
Light: Half-sunny to shady.
Soil: Humusy, well drained, moist.
Fertilizer: 30-10-10 or 14-14-14 timed-release.
Propagation: Divide in spring or fall.
Uses: Beds; borders; rock, shade, and wild gardens; pots; houseplant.

OENOTHERA
(ee-NOTH-er-ah)

Evening Primrose; Sun Drops

ONAGRACEAE; evening-primrose
family

Height/habit: Stocky, upright
to bushy, trailing, 1–3 ft.
(30–90 cm.) high/wide.
Leaves: Lance-, linear-, or
spoon-shaped, often clustered
at the base.
Flowers: Cup-shaped, 2–5 in.
(5–12.5 cm.) across; white, pink,
or yellow.

Season: Summer; *O. speciosa*
blooms spring in mild climates
and can be invasive in any
zone.
When to plant: Set transplants
when available. Cold- and heat-
tolerant zones 3–4 to 8–9.
Light: Sunny to half-sunny.
Soil: Well drained, moist.
Tolerates drought and heat
when established.
Fertilizer: 5-10-5.
Propagation: Divide or sow
seeds in spring or fall.
Uses: Beds; borders; rock, wild,
meadow, and cottage gardens.

PAEONIA
(pay-OH-nee-ah)
Peony
PAEONIACEAE; peony family

Height/habit: Herbaceous types form upright clumps, 1.5–3 ft. (45–90 cm.) high/wide (staking advised). Shrubby, woody, tree peonies grow upright, 6–12 ft. (1.8–3.6 m.) high/wide.

Leaves: Divided into leaflets or appearing palmate, 6–8 in. (15–45 cm.) across; finely cut, fernlike in *P. tenuifolia.*

Flowers: Bowl-shaped, single to double, 2–8 in. (5–20 cm.) across; all colors except blue; fragrant.

Season: Late spring through early summer.

When to plant: Set transplants when available, the roots of herbaceous peonies usually in the fall; set the growth eyes exactly 2 in. (5 cm.) deep in the soil. Cold-tolerant zones 3–4 to 8; not adapted for warmer zones since they afford insufficient hours of winter chilling. Site tree peonies so they are protected from morning sun and harsh northeast winds.

Light: Sunny.

Soil: Humusy, well drained, moist.

Fertilizer: 5-10-5.

Propagation: Divide roots (herbaceous types) in fall; take cuttings of ripe wood (tree peonies) in late fall through winter.

Uses: Beds, borders, edging, cottage gardens, cut flowers.

PAPAVER
(PAPP-ah-ver)

Perennial Poppy
PAPAVERACEAE; poppy family

Height/habit: Basal clumps of coarsely cut, hairy leaves, 1–2 ft. (30–61 cm.) high/wide, all but forgotten under the spectacular flowers, atop stems 24–40 in. (61–100 cm.) high.
Leaves: Dissected or lobed, 6–12 in. (15–30 cm.) long. They die down in summer, after flowering finishes.
Flowers: Bowl- or cup-shaped, 3–6 in. (7.5 –15 cm.) across; all reds and pinks to dark crimson to orange, salmon, and white.
Season: Early summer.
When to plant: Set transplants when available or divide roots late summer through early fall. Cold- and heat-tolerant zones 2–3 to 8; intolerant of hot, humid summers.
Light: Sunny.
Soil: Well drained, moist.
Fertilizer: 5-10-5.
Propagation: Divide in spring or late summer; take root cuttings winter through early spring.
Uses: Beds, borders, cut flowers.

PENSTEMON
(PEN-stem-on)

Beardtongue; Gulf Coast Penstemon
SCROPHULARIACEAE; figwort family

Height/habit: Tidy clumps of basal leaves, 6–12 in. (15–30 cm.) high/wide, except when the spikes of showy flowers appear in season, then 1.5–3 ft. (45–90 cm.) high/wide.
Leaves: Lance-shaped, linear, or rounded, 2–6 in. (5–15 cm.) long, sometimes evergreen.
Flowers: Tubular, 1–2 in. (2.5–5 cm.) long, in spikes above the larger leaves; all colors. Deadheading encourages a second, lesser flowering.
Season: Spring through summer.

PASSIFLORA
(pass-if-LOH-rah)

Passionflower

PASSIFLORACEAE; passionflower family

Height/habit: Small to large tendril-climbing vines, 10–30 ft. (3–9 m.); some native to North America, with fascinating flowers, often followed by showy or edible fruit.

Leaves: Variously lobed or not, some suggesting the shape of a bat wing, others of an outstretched hand, 1–8 in. (2.5–20 cm.) across.

Flowers: Complex, round, with filaments and corona, petals and sepals, 1–6 in. (2.5–15 cm.) across; white, pink, blue, red, greenish yellow, purple, or orange.

Season: Spring through summer; some hybrids ever-blooming in mild climates.

When to plant: Set transplants when available. 'Incense' and others are ground-hardy zones 5 and warmer; some species and cultivars cold-tolerant zones 8–9, thus suited only to pots in colder regions.

Light: Sunny to half-sunny.

Soil: Well drained, moist.

Fertilizer: 5-10-5.

Propagation: Take cuttings or sow seeds winter through spring.

Uses: Cover for trellis, arbor, fence, tepee in flower garden; pots.

When to plant: Set transplants when available. Choose locally adapted species sold nearby; cold- and heat-tolerant zones 3–4 to 8–9. Many are native to high, dry, and cold climates; other species, such as the Gulf Coast penstemon (*P. tenuis*), don't mind muggy heat; they bloom and go to seed before summer.

Light: Sunny.

Soil: Well drained, moist to on the dry side, some more drought-tolerant than others.

Fertilizer: 5-10-5.

Propagation: Divide in spring; take cuttings of nonflowering shoots in summer; sow seeds winter through spring.

Uses: Beds; borders; wild, meadow, and rock gardens; cut flowers.

(per-OFF-skee-ah)

Russian Sage

LABIATAE; mint family

Height/habit: Shrublike, 3–5 ft. (1–1.5 m.) high/wide.

Leaves: Egg-shaped to filigree-cut, to 2 in. (5 cm.) long; often silvery; aromatic.

Flowers: Panicles of tiny blooms resemble cloud formations in the garden; lavender or purplish blue.

Season: Late summer through fall.

When to plant: Set transplants when available. Cut back sharply in the spring to encourage annual renewal. Cold- and heat-tolerant zones 5–9.

Light: Sunny.

Soil: Well drained, moist to on the dry side.

Fertilizer: 5-10-5.

Propagation: Take stem cuttings in summer.

Uses: Beds, borders, cottage gardens.

Phlox; Moss Pink

POLEMONIACEAE; phlox family

Height/habit: Mat-forming to knee-deep spreaders to high and clump-forming, 3–48 in. (7.5–122 cm.) high, 1 ft. (30 cm.) wide or more.

Leaves: Lance- or oblong-shaped to linear, from less than 1 in. (2.5 cm.) long and needlelike in moss pink (*P. subulata*) to softly leafy, 4–6 in. (10–15 cm.) long.

Flowers: 5-lobed, tubular, to 1 in. (2.5 cm.) across, in clusters or panicles; all colors; summer phlox (*P. paniculata*) notably fragrant.

Season: Spring for native species, summer for garden phlox.

When to plant: Set transplants when available; set summer phlox root crowns while dormant, mid- to late fall. Cold- and heat-tolerant zones 4 to 8–9.

Light: Sunny to half-shady.

Soil: Well drained, moist.

Fertilizer: 5-10-5.

Propagation: Divide in spring or fall; take cuttings in summer. Seeds of hybrid phlox do not produce reliable results; it is best to deadhead phlox before seeds ripen.

Uses: Beds; borders; edging; rock, wild, and cottage gardens; cut flowers.

PHYSOSTEGIA
(feye-soss-TEE-jee-ah)

Obedient Plant

LABIATAE; mint family

Height/habit: Upright clumps, 3–4 ft. (1–1.2 m.) high x half as wide and more; colonizes.
Leaves: Lance-shaped, sharply toothed, 3–5 in. (7.5–12.5 cm.) long, set opposite along noticeably square stems.
Flowers: Tubular, lipped, and lobed, to 1 in. (2.5 cm.) long, in dense spikes; white, pink, purplish pink, lilac-tinged pink.
Season: Mid- to late summer.

When to plant: Set transplants when available. Cold- and heat-tolerant zones 3-9.
Light: Sunny to half–shady.
Soil: Humusy, well drained, moist.
Fertilizer: 5-10-5.
Propagation: Divide spring or fall (helpful for renewing congested clumps after several years); take stem cuttings in spring.
Uses: Beds, borders, wild and cottage gardens, pots, cut flowers, colonizing a moist bank or ditch.

PLATYCODON
(plat-ee-KOH-don)
Balloon Flower
CAMPANULACEAE; bellflower
family

Height/habit: Upright, narrow
to spreading clumps, 6–36 in.
(15–90 cm.) high; slow-growing.
Leaves: Egg-shaped, serrated,
to 3 in. (7.5 cm.) long, growing
in whorls up a smooth stem;
bluish green.
Flowers: Open to 5-pointed,
2-in. (5-cm.) stars growing
from balloon-shaped buds
at the terminals; there are
also doubles; blue, white, or
shell pink.
Season: Summer. Late to
sprout in spring; mark site to
avoid damage.
When to plant: Set transplants
when available. Cold- and heat-
tolerant zones 3–9.
Light: Sunny.
Soil: Well drained, moist.
Fertilizer: 5-10-5.
Propagation: Sow seed or
divide in spring; take basal
cuttings in summer.
Uses: Beds, borders, rock
and cottage gardens, pots,
cut flowers.

POLEMONIUM
(poh-lee-MOH-nee-um)

Jacob's Ladder; Greek Valerian

POLEMONIACEAE; phlox family

Height/habit: Upright to spreading, 1–2 ft. (30–61 cm.) high/wide.

Leaves: Leaflets 8–10 in. (20–25 cm.) long, paired so as to resemble ladder rungs.

Flowers: Cup- or bell-shaped, to 1 in. (2.5 cm.) across, in clusters; blue, lavender, pink, white, or yellow.

Season: Spring through summer.

When to plant: Set transplants when available. Cold- and heat-tolerant zones 3–4 to 8.

Light: Partly sunny to partly shady.

Soil: Humusy, well drained, moist.

Fertilizer: 5-10-5.

Propagation: Divide in spring; sow seeds in fall.

Uses: Bed; borders; woodland, wild, and cottage gardens; pots.

POLYGONATUM
(poh-ligg-oh-NAY-tum)
Solomon's Seal
LILIACEAE; lily family

Height/habit: Arching, unbranched stems set alternately with veined leaves and hung in spring with elegant bell flowers, averaging 2–3 ft. (61–90 cm.) high/wide.

Leaves: Broadly elliptic to lance or oval shapes, .5–6 in. (1.25–15 cm.) long.

Flowers: Resemble bells, .5 in. (1.25 cm.) long, in pairs from the leaf axils; white to greenish or lilac-tinged pink.

Season: Late spring to early summer.

When to plant: Set transplants when available. Cold- and heat-tolerant zones 4–9.

Light: Part to full shade.

Soil: Humusy, well drained, moist.

Fertilizer: 14-14-14 timed-release at planting; 5-10-5 at the start of the following season.

Propagation: Divide in spring or fall; sow seeds in fall.

Uses: Borders; shade, wild, and woodland gardens; ground cover; pots.

POLYGONUM
(poh-LIGG-oh-num)
Knotweed; Fleece Flower; Silver Lace Vine; Mexican Bamboo; Showy Bistort
POLYGONACEAE; buckwheat family

Height/habit: This genus is also known as *Periscaria*. From trailing to climbing or strongly upright, 6 in. (15 cm.) to 6–15 ft. (1.8–4.5 m.).

Leaves: Heart-shaped or oval, 1–10 in. (2.5–25 cm.) long.

Flowers: Small, reaching just .5 in. (1.25 cm.) across, often in fleecy clusters or sprays of tiny florets; white or pink, to glowing orange-crimson.

Season: Spring through fall for foliage effect, early summer for showy bistort (*P. bistorta* 'Superbum'); late summer through fall for most.

When to plant: Set transplants when available. Cold- and heat-tolerant zones 3–5 and 8–9.

Light: Sunny to partly shady.

Soil: Humusy, well drained, moist.

Fertilizer: 5-10-5.

Propagation: Divide spring or fall. *P. virginiana* (also known as *Tovara virginiana*) in the variegated-leaf variety 'Painter's Palette' produces foliar embryos that may be used to grow new plants.

Uses: Ground cover, wild gardens, pots; silver lace vine (*P. aubertii*) on fences, trellises, arbors. Mexican bamboo (*P. cuspidatum*) grows rapidly as a screen in warm weather, but roots need to be restricted by concrete or other barrier.

POTENTILLA
(poh-ten-TILL-ah)

Cinquefoil

ROSACEAE; rose family

Height/habit: Perennials
and woody plants, 6–36 in.
(15–90 cm.) high/wide.
Leaves: Compound, small,
to 1 in. (2.5 cm.) long.
Flowers: Resembling straw-
berry flower or a single rose,
5-petaled, about .75 in. (2 cm.)
across, often with showy yellow
stamens; white, yellow, red,
orange, or pink.

Season: Summer through fall.
When to plant: Set transplants
when available. Cold- and heat-
tolerant zones 4–5 to 7–8.
Light: Sunny to partly shady.
Soil: Well drained, moist.
Fertilizer: 5-10-5.
Propagation: Divide in spring
or fall; take basal cuttings in
late spring; sow seeds in spring.
Uses: Beds, borders, rock
gardens, pots.

PRIMULA
(PRIM-yew-lah)
Primrose
PRIMULACEAE; primrose family

Height/habit: Upright clumps or tidy mounds, 6–18 in. (15–45 cm.) high/wide.

Leaves: To 4 in. (10 cm.) long; rounded to lance-shaped, usually in a clump of rosettes. Some people allergic to the essential oils produced by German primrose (*P. obconica*).

Flowers: To 2 in. (5 cm.) across, alone or in clusters, rising directly from the base of the plant or from stems, to multi-levels in some, such as mature German primroses; most colors, including greens and various blues, often elaborately bicolored.

Season: Spring through early summer; winter through spring in mild-climate winters, including greenhouses.

When to plant: Set transplants when available. Cold- and heat-hardy zones 6–8 for *P. beesiana*, candelabra prim-rose (*P. bulleyana*), Japanese primrose (*P. japonica*), and *P. pulverulenta*, also called candelabra primrose; zones 5 to 8–9 for the mass-marketed *P. polyantha*, or English prim-roses. German primrose is often perennial in shady, moist gardens in zone 9.

Light: Sunny to half-sunny in cool weather, half-shady to shady at other times.

Soil: Humusy, well drained, moist.

Fertilizer: 5-10-5.

Propagation: Divide after flowering or in early fall; sow fresh seeds in summer.

Uses: Beds; borders; wild, woodland, rock, and cottage gardens; pots; cut flowers.

PULMONARIA
(pull-moh-NAY-ree-ah)

Lungwort

BORAGINACEAE; borage family

Height/habit: Self-reliant clumps 9–12 in. (22.5–30 cm.) high, spreading to twice this measurement.

Leaves: Lance- to heart-shaped, mostly from the base, 8–18 in. (20–45 cm.) long, often spotted silver with hairy stems.

Flowers: Funnel-shaped, 5-lobed, in clusters; blue, pink, red, or white.

Season: Early spring, as the foliage is emerging.

When to plant: Set transplants when available. Cold- and heat-tolerant zones 3–4 to 8.

Light: Partial to full shade.

Soil: Humusy, well drained, moist.

Fertilizer: 14-14-14 timed-release at planting time, with 5-10-5 at the beginning of the following season.

Propagation: Divide in spring or fall.

Uses: Ground cover; beds; borders; pots; wild, woodland, and cottage gardens.

RUDBECKIA
(rudd-BECK-ee-ah)

Coneflower;
Black-eyed Susan

COMPOSITAE; daisy family

Height/habit: Upright to
sprawling clumps, 2–8 ft.
(61–240 cm.) high by one-third
to half as wide; staking recommended for higher sorts, such
as *R. laciniata*, which reaches
4–8 ft. (1.2–2.4 m.).
Leaves: Rounded to lance-
shaped, deeply cut in some,
to 6 in. (15 cm.) long.
Flowers: Single or double
daisies, 2–4 in. (5–10 cm.)
across; yellow with purple-
brown to black central disks;
respond to deadheading, which
prolongs the season.
Season: Summer through fall.
When to plant: Set transplants
when available. Cold- and heat-
tolerant zones 3–4 to 9.
Light: Sunny.
Soil: Well drained, moist to on
the dry side.
Fertilizer: 5-10-5.
Propagation: Divide in spring
or fall; sow seeds in spring.
Uses: Beds; back of borders;
wild, meadow, and cottage
gardens; cut flowers.

RUELLIA
(roo-EE-lee-ah)

Wild Petunia; Mexican Petunia

ACANTHACEAE; acanthus family

Height/habit: Upright, 6–12 in. (15–30 cm.) high/wide in *R. brittoniana* 'Katie,' much higher to sprawling, 3–4 ft. (1–1.2 m.) in the wild species; high-growing Mexican petunia (*R. brittoniana*) 4–6 ft. (1.2–1.8 m.).

Leaves: Lance-shaped, 4–6 in. (10–15 cm.) long.

Flowers: Tubular, 5-lobed, 1–2 in. (2.5–5 cm.) across; blue-purple with darker veins.

Season: Spring through fall; Mexican petunia blooms mid-summer through fall. The flowers open early in the day and disappear by the afternoon, except in cooler weather.

When to plant: Set transplants when available. Cold- and heat-tolerant zones 7–9.

Light: Sunny to half-sunny.

Soil: Well drained, moist.

Fertilizer 5-10-5.

Propagation: Divide or sow seeds in spring or fall.

Uses: Beds, borders, pots, semi-wild gardens; the wild species can be invasive, but also very pretty if root run is restricted.

SALVIA
(SAL-vee-ah)

Sage

LABIATAE; mint family

Height/habit: Upright to sprawling, herbaceous to sub-shrubby, 2–8 ft. (61–240 cm.) high/wide.

Leaves: Egg-, oblong-, spoon-, or lance-shaped, 1–8 in. (2.5–20 cm.) long, prominently veined or pebbled in summer; green, gray, bluish, variegated in some; clean-scented.

Flowers: 2-lipped, often from bract of a contrasting color, 1–2 in. (2.5–5 cm.) long; most colors, but strong in blues, pinks, and reds. *S. madrensis*, a fall-flowering yellow species for mild-climate gardens (zones 8–9), gives the effect of forsythia in northern spring landscapes.

Season: Almost all year, zones 8–9 and warmer; concentrated summer for northern favorites, such as silver sage (*S. argentea*), prairie sage (*S. azurea*), mealy-cup sage (*S. farinacea*), and *S.* x *superba*.

When to plant: Set transplants when available. The species mentioned above are cold- and heat-tolerant zones 5–9; zones 7–9 there are a host of native and locally adapted species that make superb garden plants.

Light: Sunny.

Soil: Well drained, moist to on the dry side. Tolerates drought when established.

Fertilizer: 5-10-5.

Propagation: Divide herbaceous perennials or sow seeds in spring; take cuttings in midsummer.

Uses: Beds, borders, pots, wild and cottage gardens, Xeriscape.

SEDUM
(SEE-dum)

Stonecrop

CRASSULACEAE; orpine family

Height/habit: Ground-hugging, mat-forming, to 6 in. (15 cm.) high and twice to several times as wide; upright clumps in *S. spectabile*, *S. telephium*, and their offspring *S.* x 'Autumn Joy,' 15–24 in. (38–61 cm.) high/wide.

Leaves: Fleshy, pointed, cylindrical, oblong, or oval, linear or rounded, .25–6 in. (.63–15 cm.) long; various greens to bluish or gray, often with white or yellow variegation.

Flowers: Starry, tiny, reaching just .5 in. (1.25 cm.) across, in terminal clusters 2–6 in. (5–15 cm.) across; yellow, white, pink, or red to rust.

Season: Late spring, summer through fall, depending on the species. Foliage effective throughout the growing season.

When to plant: Set transplants when available. Cold- and heat-tolerant zones 3–9.

Light: Sunny.

Soil: Well drained, moist to on the dry side. Tolerates drought when established.

Fertilizer: 5-10-5.

Propagation: Divide in spring; take cuttings in summer.

Uses: Beds, borders, ground cover, rock gardens, pots.

SEMPERVIVUM
(sem-per-VEYE-vum)

Houseleek;
Live-forever

CRASSULACEAE; orpine family

Height/habit: Ground-hugging foliage in rosettes, 6–12 in. (15–30 cm.) high/wide.

Leaves: Fleshy, to 3 in. (7.5 cm.) long in dense rosettes; various greens, also bronze, red, blue- to gray-green, burgundy, lavender, purple; leaf tips often in contrasting color.

Flowers: Starry, .5–1 in. (1.25–2.5 cm.) across, in dense clusters atop an erect stem above the foliage; rose, red, purple, greenish yellow, or yellowish white.

Season: Summer; foliage attractive throughout the growing season.

When to plant: Set transplants when available. Cold- and heat-tolerant zones 5–9.

Light: Sunny.

Soil: Well drained, moist to on the dry side; drought-tolerant when established.

Fertilizer: 5-10-5.

Propagation: Take offsets in early fall or spring; sow seed in spring.

Uses: Beds, borders, rock and wall gardens, between paving stones, pots.

STACHYS
(STACK-iss)

Lamb's Ears

LABIATAE; mint family

Height/habit: *S. byzantina* mat-forming, 1–1.5 ft. (30–45 cm.) high/wide.

Leaves: Elliptical to oblong, 4–6 in. (10–15 cm.) long; white and woolly.

Flowers: Woolly spikes above or flopping over the leaves; red-purple. Fastidious gardeners often remove the buds before they open, so as to concentrate the plant's energy on the production of decorative foliage.

Season: Leaves spring through fall; often suffers die-out in summer from heat, high humidity, and overhead sprinkling.

When to plant: Set transplants when available. Cold- and heat-tolerant zones 4–8.

Light: Sunny to partly shaded.

Soil: Well drained, moist.

Fertilizer: 5-10-5.

Propagation: Divide in spring or fall.

Uses: Beds, borders, rock gardens, ground cover, pots.

STIGMAPHYLLON
(stig-mah-FILL-on)

Butterfly Vine

MALPIGHIACEAE; malpighia family

Height/habit: Twining ever-green vine to 12 ft. (3.6 m.) or more.

Leaves: Elliptical, 3–4 in. (7.5–10 cm.) long.

Flowers: Resemble butterfly orchids, each to 1.5 in. (3.7 cm.) across, in clusters of 3–7; yellow.

Season: Spring (zones 9–10), summer in cooler zones.

When to plant: Set transplants when available. Cold- and heat-tolerant zones 8–9.

Light: Sunny to half-sunny.

Soil: Well drained, moist to on the dry side.

Fertilizer: 5-10-5.

Propagation: Sow seeds in spring; take stem cuttings in summer.

Uses: Cover for trellis, fence, arbor, or tepee.

SYMPHYTUM
(sim-FEYE-tum)

Comfrey

BORAGINACEAE; borage family

Height/habit: Clump-forming, upright to sprawling, 2–4 ft. (61–122 cm.) high/wide.
Leaves: Coarse, egg- to lance-shaped, 6–10 in. (15–25 cm.) long.
Flowers: Nodding, tubular, to 1 in. (2.5 cm.) long, in branched clusters; yellow, white, blue, or pink.
Season: Spring through summer.

When to plant: Set transplants when available. Cold- and heat-tolerant zones 4–9. Most common is the herb comfrey, *S. officinale.* Showier are *S. caucasicum, S. grandiflorum,* and *S.* x *uplandicum.*
Light: Sunny to partly shady.
Soil: Humusy, well drained, moist.
Fertilizer: 5-10-5.
Propagation: Divide in spring or fall.
Uses: Beds; borders; wild, woodland, and shade gardens; pots.

THALICTRUM
(thah-LICK-trum)

Meadow Rue

RANUNCULACEAE; buttercup
family

Height/habit: Much-divided
leaves concentrated in the bottom half of the plant with
branching panicles of airy
flowers above, 3–5 ft. (1–1.5 m.)
high x half as wide.
Leaves: Small leaflets, to
1 in. (2.5 cm.); blue-green in
T. aquilegifolium. Foliage is an
asset even before the flowers
appear.
Flowers: Small blooms appear
in fluffy, showy panicles; white,
purple, lilac, or yellow.
Season: Summer.
When to plant: Set transplants
when available. Cold- and
heat-tolerant zones 5–8;
T. dasycarpum zones 5–9.
Light: Sunny to partly shaded.
Soil: Humusy, well drained,
moist.
Fertilizer: 5-10-5.
Propagation: Divide or sow
seeds in spring. Recovers slowly
from root disturbance.
Uses: Beds, borders, woodland
and wild gardens, pots.

THUNBERGIA
(thun-BERJ-ee-ah)

Blue Trumpet Vine

ACANTHACEAE; acanthus family

Height/habit: *T. grandiflora* twining evergreen vine, 20–30 ft. (6–9 m.).

Leaves: Triangular to heart-shaped, toothed, 3–8 in. (7.5–20 cm.) long.

Flowers: Lobed, tubular, to 3 in. (7.5 cm.), blooming in sprays; blue or white.

Season: Fall, winter, spring. Vines frozen back to the ground often return from the roots but take a year to come back into bloom.

When to plant: Set transplants when available. Cold- and heat-tolerant zones 8–10; elsewhere grow as a container plant placed outdoors in warm weather.

Light: Sunny to half-sunny.

Soil: Humusy, well drained, moist.

Fertilizer: 5-10-5.

Propagation: Take stem cuttings in spring or summer.

Uses: Cover for trellis, fence, arbor, or tepee; pots.

TIARELLA
(teye-ah-RELL-ah)

False Mitrewort

SAXIFRAGACEAE; saxifrage family

Height/habit: Mostly basal foliage crowned in spring by delicate flowers, 1–1.5 ft. (30–45 cm.) high/wide.

Leaves: Hairy, lobed, or divided, heart-shaped or triangular, to 3 in. (7.5 cm.), resembling those of the popular (and related) houseplant *Tolmiea*, or pickaback; evergreen except at northern hardiness limits.

Flowers: Small blooms in fuzzy spikes, 8–12 in. (20–30 cm.) long; white to pinkish.

Season: Spring through summer.

When to plant: Set transplants when available. Cold- and heat-tolerant zones 3–4 to 7–8.

Light: Shady to partly shady.

Soil: Humusy, well drained, moist.

Fertilizer: 14-14-14 timed-release at planting time.

Propagation: Divide in spring or fall; sow seed in early spring.

Uses: Beds; borders; ground cover; pots; wild, woodland, and shade gardens.

TRACHELOSPERMUM
(track-ell-OSS-per-mum)

Star Jasmine; Confederate Jasmine

APOCYNACEAE; dogbane family

Height/habit: Evergreen climber by twining stems and aerial rootlets, to 15 ft. (4.5 m.). Often trained as a bush, to 3–4 ft. (1–1.2 m.) high/wide.
Leaves: Oval, 2–3 in. (5–7.5 cm.) long.
Flowers: Starry blooms, to 1 in. (2.5 cm.) across, growing in clusters; white or pale yellow; fragrant.
Season: Spring and intermittently in summer.
When to plant: Set transplants when available. Cold- and heat-tolerant zones 8–9; *T. jasminoides* 'Madison' zones 7–10.
Light: Half-sunny to shady.
Soil: Humusy, well drained, moist.
Fertilizer: 5-10-5.
Propagation: Take cuttings in spring or summer.
Uses: Cover for trellis, fence, arbor, porch, or tepee in border.

TRADESCANTIA
(tradd-ess-KANT-ee-ah)

Spiderwort

COMMELINACEAE; spiderwort family

Height/habit: Clump-forming, upright, 1–2 ft. (30–61 cm.) high/wide.
Leaves: Narrow, similar to blades of grass, to 1 ft. (30 cm.) long.
Flowers: 3-petaled, to 1 in. (2.5 cm.) across, opening in the morning and closing by midafternoon; blue, white, pink, purple, or rose.
Season: Late spring through summer.

When to plant: Set transplants when available. Cold- and heat-tolerant zones 4–9. Cultivated hybrids of *T. ohiensis*, *T. subaspera*, and *T. virginiana*, grouped under *T.* x *andersoniana*, are best suited to the cultivated garden.
Light: Sunny to partly shady.
Soil: Humusy, well drained, moist.
Fertilizer: 5-10-5.
Propagation: Divide in spring.
Uses: Beds, borders, wild, and shade gardens, pots.

TRILLIUM
(TRILL-ee-uh)

Wake-robin

LILIACEAE; lily family

Height/habit: Clump-forming, upright, 1–1.5 ft. (30–45 cm.) high/wide.

Leaves: In groups of 3, rounded to egg-shaped, 3–6 in. (7.5–15 cm.) long; mottled yellow-green or bronze in some.

Flowers: 3-petaled or doubled, upright or nodding, 2–3 in. (5–7.5 cm.) across; white, pink, yellow, purple-red, or maroon.

Season: Spring.

When to plant: Set transplants when available. Cold- and heat-tolerant zones 3–5 to 9.

Light: Partly sunny to shady.

Soil: Humusy, well drained, moist.

Fertilizer: 5-10-5.

Propagation: Divide in early spring or late summer.

Uses: Beds; borders; wild, shade, and woodland gardens.

TROLLIUS
(TROLL-ee-uss)

Globeflower

RANUNCULACEAE; buttercup
family

Height/habit: Clumps of basal
foliage with flowers above, 1–3
ft. (30–90 cm.) high/wide.
Leaves: Fan-shaped, lobed or
divided, 2–6 in. (5–15 cm.) long.
Flowers: Globe-shaped, 1–4 in.
(2.5–10 cm.) across; yellow,
golden orange, orange-red, or
lemon.
Season: Spring through early
summer.
When to plant: Set transplants
when available. Cold- and heat-
tolerant zones 3–5 to 7.
Light: Sunny to partly shady.
Soil: Humusy, well drained,
moist to wet.
Fertilizer: 5-10-5.
Propagation: Divide in fall.
Uses: Beds, borders, bog or
wild garden, cut flowers.

VERBASCUM
(ver-BASS-kum)

Mullein

SCROPHULARIACEAE; figwort
family

Height/habit: Rosette-forming
in the first season, sending up
spires of bloom in the second,
1–2 ft. (30–61 cm.) wide by 6 ft.
(1.8 m.) high or higher in the
biennial *V. bombyciferum.*
Leaves: Oval to oblong or
broadly lance-shaped, 6–12 in.
(15–30 cm.), often densely
covered with fine hairs. Flowers
5-lobed, 1–2 in. (2.5–5 cm.)
across, in high spikes; white,
yellow, pink, purple, or orange
Deadheading the central
spike as it finishes flowering
encourages secondary spikes.
Season: Spring through
summer.
When to plant: Set transplants
when available. Cold- and heat-
tolerant zones 5–6 to 9.
Light: Sunny.
Soil: Well drained, moist to on
the dry side.
Fertilizer: 5-10-5.
Propagation: Sow seed in
spring; take root cuttings late
winter through early spring.
Uses: Beds, borders, wild
garden, pots.

VERONICA
(ver-ON-ick-ah)

Speedwell

SCROPHULARIACEAE; figwort family

Height/habit: Prostrate, trailing, or mat-forming to upright clumps (staking helps), 6–12 in. (15–30 cm.) to 1.5–3 ft. (45–90 cm.) high/wide.

Leaves: Oblong, egg- to lance-shaped, often toothed, 1–3 in. (2.5–7.5 cm.) long.

Flowers: Saucer-shaped, small, in dense spikes; blue, white, pink, or violet-blue.

Season: Late spring, summer, fall.

When to plant: Set transplants when available. Cold- and heat-tolerant zones 4–8.

Light: Sunny.

Soil: Well drained, moist.

Fertilizer: 5-10-5.

Propagation: Divide in spring or fall; take cuttings in summer.

Uses: Beds, borders, rock and wall gardens, pots.

VIOLA
(veye-OH-lah)

Violet

VIOLACEAE; violet family

Height/habit: Upright to spreading, tufted or stemmed, 4–12 in. (10–30 cm.) high/wide.
Leaves: Rounded, lance-, heart-, or ivy-shaped, 1–2 in. (2.5–5 cm.) across.
Flowers: Single or double, 1–2 in. (2.5–5 cm.) across; blue, lilac, white, violet, yellow, ruby red, mauve purple; some fragrant, notably *V. odorata*.
Season: Winter through spring in mild climates; primarily spring in colder regions.
When to plant: Set transplants when available. Cold- and heat-tolerant zones 3–5 to 8–9. Widely adapted, some becoming outright weeds, others indispensable as edgings and ground covers.
Light: Sunny to partly shady.
Soil: Humusy, well drained, moist.
Fertilizer: 5-10-5.
Propagation: Divide in spring or fall; sow seeds or take cuttings in spring or summer.
Uses: Beds; borders; ground cover; wild, shade, and rock gardens; pots; cut flowers.

VITEX
(VEYE-tex)

Chaste Tree

VERBENACEAE; verbena family

Height/habit: Though technically shrubs or small trees that can reach 10–15 ft. (3–4.5 m.) high/wide, these plants can often be cut to the ground in spring so that relatively small, compact new season's growth produces bloom at a welcome time in the garden.

Leaves: Compound into 5–7 leaflets, to 4 in. (10 cm.) long. Grayish green (variegated white in some) and aromatic.

Flowers: Very small in showy terminal clusters to 4–8 in. (10–20 cm.) long; blue, white, pink, lilac, or lavender; fragrant.

Season: Summer, earlier in warmest zones.

When to plant: Set transplants when available. Cold- and heat-tolerant zones 6–7 to 9–10.

Light: Sunny.

Soil: Well drained, moist. Tolerates drought when established.

Fertilizer: 5-10-5.

Propagation: Take cuttings or layer in spring or summer.

Uses: Beds, back of borders, wild or cottage gardens, pots.

YUCCA
(YUCK-ah)
Spanish Dagger
AGAVACEAE; agave family

Height/habit: Rosette or sword-shaped leaves, above which flowers rise on woody spike, 4–8 ft. (1.2–2.4 m.) high/wide.
Leaves: Narrow daggers, .5 in. (1.25 cm.) wide x up to 3 ft. (90 cm.) long in *Y. glauca*; also varying in succulence and fiber content, from relatively flexuous to quite hard; from blue- to yellow-green, some variegated lengthwise with white to pale yellow; evergreen, but some deciduous.
Flowers: Pyramidal spires of pendant bells 2–4 in. (5–10 cm.) across; white or purple; fragrant.
Season: Spring through summer.
When to plant: Set transplants when available.
Light: Sunny.
Soil: Well drained, moist to on the dry side; very drought-tolerant when established.
Fertilizer: 5-10-5.
Propagation: Take root cuttings or divide spring or fall.
Uses: Beds, borders, Xeriscape, pots, cut flowers.

Chapter Three
Troubleshooting Guide for Perennials

The best way to keep a garden trouble-free is to prevent problems from arising in the first place. Ensure that any plants you obtained are as healthy as possible, and keep the garden cleaned of debris and weeds, which provide convenient cover for insects. Even the most diligent gardener experiences problems, however, such as the following:

No blooms. This signals the need for more light, more water or fertilizer, or possibly more cold (peonies will not bloom unless they have sufficient hours of chilling in winter, usually in zones 8 and colder). Sometimes this is a sign that the plants have lived for too long in one spot, without replenishment of the soil and without division and thinning out of other plant competition.

Insects clustered on new growth. These are probably aphids and can be knocked off with stiff streams of water from the hose or treated with insecticidal soap or Neem tree sprays (a traditional Indian bug repellent).

White insects clustered on main stems from the ground up. These are doubtlessly mealybugs. Spray weekly and thoroughly with insecticidal soap or Neem tree sprays.

Powdery white spots on leaves. Powdery mildew attacks numerous perennials, especially summer phlox. This usually happens late in the summer when nights turn cool and days remain warm and dry. The condition can be treated by applying fungicide.

Tiny white flies around plant; lower leaves moldy. Spray weekly with insecticidal soap or other spray labeled specifically for use against white flies. The plant will outgrow the sooty mold; it cannot be removed.

Generally poor or weak growth. The plant needs more light, water, and nutrients. Avoid planting perennials where the soil is filled with tree and shrub roots. In such situations it may be better to grow selected perennials in containers.

Chapter Four
Bringing Perennials Into Your Home

Container-grown perennials are a perfect way of enjoying these plants indoors. Gallon-size or larger service pots can be dressed for indoors by slipping each inside a woven basket, cachepot, or earthen container, with some sheet moss to carpet any bare surface soil.

Perennial flowers and vines are also a seemingly endless source of fragrant blooms and fresh foliage for arrangements. Whether creating a casual bouquet for a milk bottle on the porch or a formal centerpiece for the dining room, here are some delightful suggestions:

❧ Aster with irises, snapdragon, marigold, lily or zinnia

❧ Chrysanthemum with dianthus (a long-lasting combination)

❧ Country-style combinations of delphinium with gerbera, snapdragon, purple coneflower

❧ Irises in Oriental-style ikebana arrangements

❧ Liatris as framework flower in large-scale designs

❧ Phlox with tulips and snapdragons

❧ Coralbells with miniature roses and violets

For everlastings arrangements and potpourri, the following air-dried flowers and seed heads are recommended:

❧ Delphinium for brilliant color in potpourri

❧ False goat's beard for unique texture of dried flowers in potpourri

❧ Peony petals for color and heavenly scent in potpourri

❧ Yarrow with false indigo dried seed heads

❧ Globe thistle with strawflowers

Bibliography

Bailey, Liberty Hyde, and Ethel Zoe Bailey; revised and expanded by the staff of the L.H. Bailey Hortorium. 1976. *Hortus Third.* New York: Macmillan Publishing Co.

Bailey, Ralph; McDonald, Elvin; Good Housekeeping Editors. 1972. *The Good Housekeeping Illustrated Encyclopedia of Gardening.* New York: Book Division, Hearst Magazines.

Graf, Alfred Byrd. 1992. *Hortica.* New Jersey: Roehrs Co.

Greenlee, John. 1992. *The Encyclopedia of Ornamental Grasses.* Pennsylvania: Rodale Press.

Heriteau, Jacqueline, and Charles B. Thomas. 1994. *Water Gardens.* Boston/New York: Houghton Mifflin Co.

Hobhouse, Penelope, and Elvin McDonald, Consulting Editors. 1994. *Gardens of the World: The Art & Practice of Gardening.* New York: Macmillan Publishing Co.

Hobhouse, Penelope. 1994. *On Gardening.* New York: Macmillan Publishing Co.

McDonald, Elvin. 1993. *The New Houseplant: Bringing the Garden Indoors.* New York: Macmillan Publishing Co.

McDonald, Elvin. 1995. *The Color Garden Series: Red, White, Blue, Yellow.* San Francisco: Collins Publishers.

McDonald, Elvin. 1995. *The Traditional Home Book of Roses.* Des Moines: Meredith Books.

Mulligan, William C. 1992. *The Adventurous Gardener's Sourcebook of Rare and Unusual Plants.* New York: Simon & Schuster.

Mulligan, William C. 1995. *The Lattice Gardener.* New York: Macmillan Publishing Co.

River Oaks Garden Club. 1989. Fourth Revised Edition. *A Garden Book for Houston.* Houston: Gulf Publishing Co.

Royal Horticultural Society, The; Clayton, John, revised by John Main. Third Edition. 1992. *Pruning Ornamental Shrubs.* London: Cassell Educational Ltd.

Scanniello, Stephen, and Tania Bayard. 1994 *Climbing Roses.* New York: Prentice Hall.

Schinz, Marina, and Gabrielle van Zuylen. 1991. *The Gardens of Russell Page.* New York: Stewart, Tabori & Chang.

Sedenko, Jerry. 1991. *The Butterfly Garden.* New York: Villard Books.

Sunset Books and Sunset Magazine. 1995. *Sunset Western Garden Book.* Menlo Park: Sunset Publishing Co.

Woods, Christopher. 1992. *Encyclopedia of Perennials.* New York: Facts On File, Inc.

Yang, Linda. 1995. *The City & Town Gardener: A Handbook for Planting Small Spaces and Containers.* New York: Random House.

Resources

Jacques Amand
P.O. Box 59001
Potomac, MD 20859
free catalog; all kinds of bulbs

Amaryllis, Inc.
P.O. Box 318
Baton Rouge, LA 70821
free list; hybrid Hippeastrum

Antique Rose Emporium
Rt. 5, Box 143
Brenham, TX 77833
catalog $5; old roses, also peren-
nials, ornamental grasses

Appalachian Gardens
Box 82
Waynesboro, PA 17268
catalog $2; uncommon
woodies

B & D Lilies
330 "P" St.
Port Townsend, WA 98368
catalog $3; garden lilies

The Banana Tree, Inc.
715 Northampton St.
Easton, PA 18042
catalog $3; seeds of exotics

Beaver Creek Nursery
7526 Pelleaux Rd.
Knoxville, TN 37938
catalog $1; uncommon
woodies

Kurt Bluemel
2740 Greene Lane
Baldwin, MD 21013
catalog $2; ornamental grasses,
perennials

Bluestone Perennials
7237 Middle Ridge
Madison, OH 44057
free catalog; perennials

Borboleta Gardens
15980 Canby Ave., Rt. 5
Faribault, MN 55021
catalog $3; bulbs, tubers,
corms, rhizomes

Bovees Nursery
1737 S.W. Coronado
Portland, OR 97219
catalog $2; uncommon
woodies

Brand Peony Farms
P.O. Box 842
St. Cloud, MN 56302
free catalog; peonies

Breck's
6523 N. Galena Rd.
Peoria, IL 61632
free catalog; all kinds
of bulbs

Briarwood Gardens
14 Gully Lane, R.F.D. 1
East Sandwich, MA 02537
list $1; azaleas,
rhododendrons

Brudy's Tropical Exotics
P.O. Box 820874
Houston, TX 77282
catalog $2; seeds,
plants of exotics

W. Atlee Burpee Co.
300 Park Ave.
Warminster, PA 18974
free catalog; seeds, plants,
bulbs, supplies, wide selection

Busse Gardens
5873 Oliver Ave., S.W.
Cokato, MN 55321
catalog $2; perennials

Camellia Forest Nursery
125 Carolina Forest
Chapel Hill, NC 27516
list $1; uncommon
woodies

Canyon Creek Nursery
3527 DIY Creek Rd.
Oroville, CA 95965
catalog $2; silver-leaved plants

Carroll Gardens
Box 310
Westminster, MD 21158
catalog $2; perennials,
woodies, herbs

Coastal Gardens
4611 Socastee Blvd.
Myrtle Beach, SC 29575
catalog $3; perennials

The Cummins Garden
22 Robertsville Rd.
Marlboro, NJ 07746
catalog $2; azaleas,
rhododendrons, woodies

The Daffodil Mart
Rt. 3, Box 794
Gloucester, VA 23061
list $1; Narcissus specialists,
other bulbs

Daylily World
P.O. Box 1612
Sanford, FL 32772
catalog $5; all kinds of
Hemerocallis

deJager Bulb Co.
Box 2010
So. Hamilton, MA 01982
free list; all kinds of bulbs

Tom Dodd's Rare Plants
9131 Holly St.
Semmes, AL 36575
list $1; trees, shrubs,
extremely select

Far North Gardens
16785 Harrison Rd.
Livonia, MI 48154
catalog $2; primulas,
other perennials

Flora Lan Nursery
9625 Northwest
Roy Forest Grove, OR 97116
free catalog; uncommon
woodies

Forest Farm
990 Tetherow Rd.
Williams, OR 97544-9599
catalog $3; uncommon
woodies in small sizes

Fox Hill Farm
P.O. Box 7
Parma, MI 49269
catalog $1; all kinds of herbs

Howard B. French
Box 565
Pittsfield, VT 05762
free catalog; bulbs

Gardens of the Blue Ridge
Box 10
Pineola, NC 28662
catalog $3; wildflowers
and ferns

D. S. George Nurseries
2515 Penfield Rd.
Fairport, NY 14450
free catalog; clematis

Girard Nurseries
Box 428
Geneva, OH 44041
free catalog; uncommon
woodies

Glasshouse Works
Greenhouses
Church St., Box 97
Stewart, OH 45778
catalog $2; exotics for
containers

Gossler Farms Nursery
1200 Weaver Rd.
Springfield, OR 97477
list $2; uncommon
woodies

Greenlee Ornamental Grasses
301 E. Franklin Ave.
Pomona, CA 91766
catalog $5; native and
ornamental grasses

Greer Gardens
1280 Goodpasture Island Rd.
Eugene, OR 97401
catalog $3; uncommon
woodies, especially
Rhododendron

Grigsby Cactus Gardens
2354 Bella Vista Dr.
Vista, CA 92084
catalog $2; cacti and
other succulents

Growers Service Co.
10118 Crouse Rd.
Hartland, MI 48353
list $1; all kinds of bulbs

Heirloom Old Garden Roses
24062 N.E. Riverside Dr.
St. Paul, OR 97137
catalog $5; old garden, English,
and winter-hardy roses

Holbrook Farm and Nursery
Box 368
Fletcher, NC 28732
free catalog; woodies and
other select plants

J. L. Hudson, Seedsman
P.O. Box 1058
Redwood City, CA 94064
catalog $1; nonhybrid flowers,
vegetables

Jackson and Perkins
1 Rose Lane
Medford, OR 97501
free catalog; roses, perennials

Kartuz Greenhouses
1408 Sunset Dr.
Vista, CA 92083
catalog $2; exotics
for containers

Klehm Nursery
Rt. 5, Box 197 Penny Rd.
So. Barrington, IL 60010
catalog $5; peonies,
Hemerocallis, hostas,
perennials

M. & J. Kristick
155 Mockingbird Rd.
Wellsville, PA 17365
free catalog; conifers

Lamb Nurseries
Rt. 1, Box 460B
Long Beach, WA 98631
catalog $1; perennials

Las Pilitas Nursery
Star Rt., Box 23
Santa Margarita, CA 93453
catalog $6; California natives

Lauray of Salisbury
432 Undermountain Rd.
Rt. 41
Salisbury, CT 06068
catalog $2; exotics
for containers

Lilypons Water Gardens
6800 Lilypons Rd.
P.O. Box 10
Buckeystown, MD 21717
catalog $5; aquatics

Limerock Ornamental Grasses
R.D. 1, Box 111
Port Matilda, PA 16870
list $3

Logee's Greenhouses
141 North St.
Danielson, CT 06239
catalog $3; exotics for
containers

Louisiana Nursery
Rt. 7, Box 43
Opelousas, LA 70570
catalogs $3–$6;
uncommon woodies,
perennials

Lowe's Own Root Roses
6 Sheffield Rd.
Nashua, NH 03062
list $5; old roses

McClure & Zimmerman
Box 368
Friesland, WI 53935
free catalog; all kinds of bulbs

Mellinger's
2310 W. South Range Rd. North
Lima, OH 44452
free catalog; all kinds of plants

Merry Gardens
Upper Mechanic St., Box 595
Camden, ME 04843
catalog $2; herbs,
pelargoniums, cultivars
of Hedera helix

Milaeger's Gardens
4838 Douglas Ave.
Racine, WI 53402
catalog $1; perennials

Moore Miniature Roses
2519 E. Noble Ave.
Visalia, CA 93292
catalog $1; all kinds of
miniature roses

Niche Gardens
1111 Dawson Rd.
Chapel Hill, NC 27516
catalog $3; perennials

Nichols Garden Nursery
1190 N. Pacific Highway
Albany, OR 97321
free catalog; uncommon
edibles, flowers, herbs

Nor'East Miniature Roses
Box 307
Rowley, MA 01969
free catalog

North Carolina State University
Arboretum
Box 7609
Raleigh, NC 27695
Propagation guide for woody
plants and lists of plants in
the arboretum, $10; member-
ship permits participation in
worthy plant propagation
and dissemination.

Oakes Daylilies
8204 Monday Rd.
Corryton, TN 37721
free catalog; all kinds
of Hemerocallis

Geo. W. Park Seed Co.
Box 31
Greenwood, SC 29747
free catalog; all kinds of seeds,
plants, and bulbs

Plants of the Southwest
Agua Fria, Rt. 6,
Box 11A
Santa Fe, NM 87501
catalog $3.50

Roses of Yesterday and Today
802 Brown's Valley Rd.
Watsonville, CA 95076
catalog $3 third class,
$5 first; old roses

Roslyn Nursery
211 Burrs Lane
Dix Hills, NY 11746
catalog $3; woodies, perennials

John Scheepers, Inc.
P.O. Box 700
Bantam, CT 06750
free catalog; all kinds of bulbs

Seymour's Selected Seeds
P.O. Box 1346
Sussex, VA 23884-0346
free catalog; English
cottage garden seeds

Shady Oaks Nursery
112 10th Ave. S.E.
Waseca, MN 56093
catalog $2.50; hostas, ferns,
wildflowers, shrubs

Siskiyou Rare Plant Nursery
2825 Cummings Rd.
Medford, OR 97501
catalog $2; alpines

Anthony J. Skittone
1415 Eucalyptus
San Francisco, CA 94132
catalog $2; unusual bulbs,
especially from South Africa

Sonoma Horticultural Nursery
3970 Azalea Ave.
Sebastopol, CA 95472
catalog $2; azaleas,
rhododendrons

Spring Hill Nurseries
110 W. Elm St.
Tipp City, OH 45371
free catalog; perennials,
woodies, roses

Sunnybrook Farms Homestead
9448 Mayfield Rd.
Chesterland, OH 44026
catalog $2; perennials, herbs

Surry Gardens
P.O. Box 145
Surry, ME 04684
free list; perennials, vines,
grasses, wild garden

Terrapin Springs Nursery
Box 7454
Tifton, GA 31793
list $1; uncommon
woodies

Thompson & Morgan
Box 1308
Jackson, NJ 08527
free catalog; all kinds
of seeds

Transplant Nursery
1586 Parkertown Rd.
Lavonia, GA 30553
catalog $1; azaleas,
rhododendrons

Twombly Nursery, Inc.
163 Barn Hill Rd.
Monroe, CT 06468
list $4; uncommon
woodies

Van Engelen, Inc.
Stillbrook Farm
313 Maple St.
Litchfield, CT 06759
free catalog; all kinds
of bulbs

Andre Viette Farm & Nursery
Rt. 1, Box 16
Fishersville, VA 22939
catalog $3; perennials,
ornamental grasses

Washington Evergreen Nursery
Box 388
Leicester, NC 28748
catalog $2; conifers

Wayside Gardens
One Garden Lane
Hodges, SC 29695
free catalog; all kinds
of bulbs, woodies,
perennials, vines

We-Du Nursery
Rt. 5, Box 724
Marion, NC 28752
catalog $2; uncommon
woodies, perennials

White Flower Farm
Box 50
Litchfield, CT 06759
catalog $5; woodies,
perennials, bulbs

Whitman Farms
3995 Gibson Rd., N.W.
Salem, OR 97304
catalog $1; woodies,
edibles

Gilbert H. Wild and Son, Inc.
Sarcoxie, MO 64862
catalog $3; perennials, peonies,
iris, Hemerocallis

Winterthur Plant Shop
Winterthur, DE 19735
free list; uncommon woodies

Woodlanders
1128 Colleton Ave.
Aiken, SC 29801
catalog $2; woodies,
hardy Passiflora

Yucca Do
P.O. Box 655
Waller, TX 77484
catalog $3; woodies, perennials

Credits

Thanks to the gardeners and institutions who permitted me to photograph perennial flowers and gardens:

American Horticultural Society, River Farm, Alexandria, VA

Antique Rose Emporium, Brenham, TX

Atlanta Botanic Garden, Atlanta, GA

Jean Atwater, Spokane, WA

Ernesta and Fred Ballard, Philadelphia, PA

Berkshire Botanic Garden, Stockbridge, MA

Bourton House and Gardens, England

British Columbia, University of, Botanic Garden, Vancouver, BC

Brooklyn Botanic Garden, Brooklyn, NY

Francis Cabot, La Malbaie, Quebec

Conservatory Garden in Central Park, New York, NY

Mr. and Mrs. Stuart Crowner, Pasadena, CA

Denmans Garden, John Brooks, England

Dixon Gallery and Gardens, Memphis, TN

C. Z. Guest, Old Westbury, NY

Joshua's Native Plants and Garden Antiques, Houston, TX

Lamb Nurseries, Spokane, WA

Live Oak Gardens, New Iberia, LA

Logee's Greenhouses, Danielson, CT

Longue Vue Gardens, New Orleans, LA

Longwood Gardens, Kennett Square, PA

Frederick and Mary Ann McGourty, Norfolk, CT

Mercer Arboretum and Botanic Gardens, Humble, TX

Lynden and Leigh Miller, Sharon, CT

Minnesota, University of, Landscape Arboretum, Canhassen, MN

Minnesota, University of, School of Business, St. Paul, MN

Montreal Botanic Garden, Montreal, Quebec

National Wildflower Research Center, Austin, TX

The New York Botanical Garden, Bronx, NY

Old Westbury Gardens, Old Westbury, NY

Geo. W. Park Seed Co., Inc., Greenwood, SC

Peckerwood Gardens, Waller, TX

Pier 39, San Francisco, CA

Planting Fields Arboretum, Oyster Bay, NY

Plum Creek Farm, Sharon, CT

Royal Botanical Garden at Kew, London, England

George Schoellkopf, CT

Sissinghurst Castle Gardens, Kent, England

Strybing Arboretum, San Francisco, CA

Wakehurst Gardens, England

U.S.D.A. Plant Hardiness Zone Map

Average Annual Minimum Temperature

Temperature (°C)	Zone	Temperature (°F)
-45.6 and below	1	below -50
-45.6 and -45.5	2a	-45 to -50
-40.0 to -42.7	2b	-40 to -45
-37.3 to -40.0	3a	-35 to -40
-34.5 to -37.2	3b	-30 to -35
-31.7 to -34.4	4a	-25 to -30
-28.9 to -31.6	4b	-20 to -25
-26.2 to -28.8	5a	-15 to -20
-23.4 to -26.1	5b	-10 to -15
-20.6 to -23.3	6a	-5 to -10
-17.8 to -20.5	6b	0 to -5
-15.0 to -17.7	7a	5 to 0
-12.3 to -15.0	7b	10 to 5
-9.5 to -12.2	8a	15 to 10
-6.7 to -9.4	8b	20 to 15
-3.9 to -6.6	9a	25 to 20
-1.2 to -3.8	9b	30 to 25
1.6 to -1.1	10a	35 to 30
4.4 to 1.7	10b	40 to 45
4.5 and above	11	40 and above

This map, issued by the United States Department of Agriculture, lists average annual minimum temperatures for each zone. It relates directly to the cold-hardiness of plants, but does not address the other extreme, high temperatures. Special considerations with regard to these matters are noted as appropriate throughout the pages of this book.
A new map, in preparation by the U.S.D.A. in cooperation with the American Horticultural Society, will treat equally matters of hot and cold and their effect on plants.